The Kennedy Center

Enjoy the Tour!

Barbara Morris

The Kennedy Center

An Insider's Guide to Washington's Liveliest Memorial

Barbara Bradlyn Morris

EPM Publications, Inc.
McLean, Virginia

Library of Congress Cataloging-in-Publication Data

Morris, Barbara Bradlyn.
    The Kennedy Center : an insider's guide to Washington's liveliest
memorial / Barbara Bradlyn Morris.
        p.   cm.
    Includes index.
    ISBN 0-939009-79-X
    1. John F. Kennedy Center for the Performing Arts (U.S.)
I. Title.
PN1588.W3M67   1994
791'.09753--dc20   94-1836
                                                                        CIP

EPM Publications, Inc., 1003 Turkey Run Road
    McLean, VA 22101
Printed in the United States of America
First Printing, March 1994
Floor Plan: Stephen Kraft
Book Design: Konetzka Design Group

Cover: The bronze bust of President Kennedy by Robert Berks
is the focal point of the Grand Foyer.

Frontispiece: Streaks of tail lights mark the arrival of
theatergoers at the front plaza.

Contents

*Dedicated with joy and love to my husband,
Ward, and my parents, Martha and Peter*

With thanks to God

Foreword

As one of more than one hundred volunteer tour
guides at the Kennedy Center, I love to see the faces
of visitors light up when I lead them beneath sparkling
chandeliers, through grand halls and into opulent theaters and lounges. It's especially rewarding when they
ask questions, murmur in appreciation of the beauty of
the art or chuckle at an amusing anecdote.

As you can imagine, in an hour's tour, a guide can
only touch on the highlights of the Center's history
and its treasury of gifts from other countries. One hour
simply isn't time enough to tell the fascinating stories
behind the gifts or to convey the visitors' responses to
the Center's size and splendor. There isn't time to describe the myriad performances and educational programs that go on day after day. The intent of this
book, in short, is to tell the Kennedy Center story
more fully by taking you on a tour similar to the daily
tours, but with more background details.

I hope that you'll get to know the Center a little
better, view its treasury of art with a fresh, new vision
and learn about its extensive young people's programs
that magically weave education with top-flight entertainment. I also hope you'll sense the friendly, welcoming atmosphere created by staff and volunteers
alike, and come to know how this unusual memorial
works as a culture center as well as a classroom for the
entire country.

Introduction

Of all the memorial buildings in Washington, D.C., whose parks and plazas are dotted with monuments to past presidents, only The John F. Kennedy Center for the Performing Arts is a "living" memorial. Unlike the lovely but solemn monuments to Presidents Jefferson and Lincoln which resemble the marble temples of ancient Greece, the Kennedy Center resounds with life. There is the laughter and chatter of thousands of theater-goers, school children and tourists eager to explore the Center's theaters, restaurants and gift shops. And that's just on this side of the footlights.

On stage, the finest artists in the world perform in dramas, comedies, musicals, chamber music concerts, symphonies, operas, ballets, folk dances, jazz bands, modern dance and choral groups. Behind the scenes stagehands, designers, electricians, make-up artists and wardrobe mistresses scurry about helping to create theater magic. Clearly, the Kennedy Center is a lively monument.

A quiet moment under the willow trees on the River Terrace.

Designed by Edward Durrell Stone in a clean-lined, rectangular shape, the white marble building is bordered by a colonnade of 66 slim, 60-foot-tall gilded pillars. The look is sleek, a modern counterpoint to the classical columns that grace much of Washington's architecture. A tree-lined marble plaza fronts the Center where American flags whip in the breeze from the Potomac River. At the rear, on the terrace overlooking the river, willow trees sway gracefully above a thick carpet of English ivy. Crystal-clear fountains, lighted at night, are reflected in the tall glass doors which open onto the Grand Foyer, the sparkling main lobby.

The Kennedy Center did not start as a memorial to the slain president. Originally it was intended to become a much-needed national center for the performing arts. But, as you'll discover on the following pages, time and fate altered those plans.

1 A Giant Stride into the Cultural Age

It was embarrassing. Here it was the 1950s. Washington, D.C. was the most influential city in the world, yet many foreign diplomats stationed here actually regarded it as a hardship post.

The reason? A distressing culture shortage. Most world class performers avoided the city simply because it lacked the kinds of theaters that could do justice to their talents. Fortunately, one of the people who recognized this lack was President Eisenhower. The United States had come of age, he felt, and needed to show the world our artistic talents, not just our "broad lands, great cities and humming factories." Turning thought into action, he formed a commission to study the ways and means of building a national arts center. Based on the commission's recommendation, the President signed the National Cultural Center Act in 1958.

Flanked by scaffolding, the bust of President Kennedy is securely in place a few days before the grand opening of the Center. In these last moments, sculptor Robert Berks reflects on his massive work.

Could anyone then possibly have guessed what a tremendous impact that Act would come to have on cultural life in Washington? Or on artistic life across the country?

The Act had four basic features. (1) It authorized the construction of a national center dedicated to the performing arts. (2) It spelled out the center's artistic mandate: to present a wide variety of both classical and contemporary performing arts. (3) It specified that the center was to offer educational programs for all ages. (4) Finally—of great significance—it stated that the center was to be independent, self-sustaining and privately funded.

Quite a mandate. A mammoth task of fund-raising lay ahead, but at least the first big step had been taken.

Over the next thirteen years, until the grand opening in 1971, the project moved fitfully. Two steps forward, one step back. It didn't help that so many committees were involved—commissions on trade, fine arts, public works, for example. So many hurdles lay in the way that it's a wonder the building was ever completed.

One of the first problems was where to build. Many sites were considered, then turned down for a variety of reasons. There were conflicts with other planned buildings, problems in land acquisition, traffic flow issues and drainage problems. It's ironic that the center finally wound up in the area called Foggy Bottom, the 200-year-old nickname that refers to the swampy land along the Potomac. Critics of the center—you could almost hear them chuckling—predicted that the building would sink into the ooze. The problems were so great that Richard Coe, drama critic of *The Washington Post* wryly remarked that, "The Perils of Pauline pale beside the birth pangs of the Kennedy Center."

The man who faced these problems down time and again was Board Chairman Roger L. Stevens, truly a Renaissance man whose name is almost synonymous with the Kennedy Center for which he has worked tirelessly—and voluntarily—for almost 30 years.

In addition to being a real estate investment businessman, (he negotiated the 1951 sale of the Empire State Building), Mr. Stevens was a major theatrical producer in New York and London, producing or co-producing more than 200 plays including *West Side Story, Tea and Sympathy, A Man for All Seasons, Bus Stop, A Few Good Men, Shadowlands* and *The Cocktail Hour.* His combined interests in real estate and the arts made him the perfect choice to take charge of fund-raising and programming for the National Cultural Center (which became the Kennedy Center). President Kennedy appointed him to the position in 1961. At one point during the construction period when it looked as though the backward steps might outnumber the forward ones, Mr. Stevens hustled over to the building site and declared to the press and public at large, "I won't stop until I produce a building for you!" With that, he hopped up on a derrick and grabbed its controls to dramatize his vow.

One problem that wouldn't go away was cost. Edward Durrell Stone, the architect selected by the Board of Trustees, drew up a fantastic plan that included riverside entrances for theater-goers arriving in special barges. It sounded grand. It should have—at an estimated cost of $75–100 million!

Mr. Stevens suggested that Mr. Stone cut back a bit. More than just a bit. More like half, actually.

Mr. Stone's modified design made the most of the hallmark of his work: clean, elegant lines of a handsome yet practical building. Its cost was estimated at $31 million—and that became the fund-raising goal.

The fund drive began in November 1962 with a closed circuit television gala called American Pageant of the Arts. President and Mrs. Kennedy introduced the gala which starred a dazzling array of performers including host Leonard Bernstein, Pablo Casals, Dorothy Kirsten, Marian Anderson, Benny Goodman, Yo-Yo Ma, Bob Newhart, Richard Tucker, Harry Belafonte, Hal Holbrook, Colleen Dewhurst, Maria Tallchief, Danny Kaye, Van Cliburn, and others. Incredibly, this star-studded gala raised only half a million dollars.

With his typical energy and determination *cum* charm, President Kennedy tackled the task of fund-raising at special White House luncheons and dinners for prominent business men and women. He talked plainly, putting the prestige of his office solidly behind the fund drive, and reminded his influential guests of the renowned performing arts centers in other countries. "But here in the world's greatest capital," he declared, "we have nothing!"

Finally, the fund drive got wider publicity when the President named his wife and Mrs. Eisenhower as honorary co-chairwomen. Momentum picked up; sizeable donations began streaming in. Even school kids got into the act with scrap paper drives that raised $20,000.

Then, on November 22, 1963, President Kennedy was assassinated.

In January 1964, while the stunned nation still mourned, Congress passed an act—which President Johnson immediately signed—that called for the performing arts center to be named in honor of the slain president. The law made clear that this was to be a very special building, the one and only memorial to President Kennedy in the nation's capital.

It was a moving moment in December 1965, when President Johnson broke ground for the Kennedy Center, turning the first shovelful of earth with the same gold-plated spade that had broken the ground for the Lincoln Memorial in 1914 and the Jefferson Memorial in 1938.

The next six years of construction were difficult years of work-delaying labor disputes, spiraling building costs and constant fund-raising efforts. The original goal of $31 million covered only the building. The price of the 17-acre plot of land and underground garage hiked the cost to $50 million. Added expense came with the need for insulating the building from jet noise from near-by National Airport, for reinforcing the ceilings to take the weight of huge chandeliers and for adapting stage floors to meet the requirements of ballet. The final figure rose to over $70 million.

Private gifts came to $34 million. Congress authorized $23 million when the Center became a presidential memorial and the Treasury authorized $20.4 million in revenue bonds. Repayment began in 1987.

Because of the dual role for the Center as both the nation's performing arts arena and memorial to President Kennedy, its funding structure was to be unique. As it does for all presidential memorials, the National Park Service would provide the maintenance and security and would cover utility costs for the building. The Center itself, however, would be responsible for presenting performing arts programming; the funds would be raised chiefly from performance income and private donations.

Heartwarming responses came from corporations, individuals and foreign governments who offered gifts of building supplies and furnishings as well as priceless objects of art, for which they commissioned their finest artists. Without these gifts the Center probably would not have been built, according to Roger Meersman, theater historian and critic. In fact, things came right down to the wire. In his history of the Center, Dr.

Meersman relates the dramatic, photo-finish end of the fund drive. If the Kennedy Center trustees were to receive matching government funds, they had to raise $15.5 million from private sources. However, they had to raise it by June 30, 1965—a tight deadline which looked impossible to meet.

And then, on June 29, only a few hours before the deadline, the people of Italy presented their gift of $1,168,000 worth of marble. This, along with the millions in gifts from other countries, saved the day.

Finally, construction began in January 1967. The steel girders rose, and a landmark step was reached the next January when the first major segment of construction on the Concert Hall was completed. It was celebrated by hoisting an 11-foot high replica of a bass viol to the top of the girders.

Eight months later the final girder of the building was put in place. Traditionally, this construction milestone is celebrated by raising a flag over the girders in a "topping out" ceremony. The Center was "topped out" instead with giant-size masks of Comedy and Tragedy. This was the "official" celebration. Unofficially, the steel workers had already celebrated the placement of the final girder with a beer party.

Even before it opened, the Kennedy Center had become a showcase for art. Its first paintings—children's views of Washington—were displayed on the wooden fence around the construction site. The paintings began simply as an amusing project for a children's art class at the Corcoran Art Gallery, but the paintings were so charming that the project blossomed. Volunteers—Friends of the Kennedy Center—got in touch with government officials worldwide, and soon they received gaily painted panels from children in 41 states and 22 foreign countries. With so many hands working on it, the fence was nicknamed "The Tom Sawyer Fence."

At last, in 1971, the Center was ready to welcome an excited and curious public. With five acoustically excellent theaters ranging in size from 224 to 2,750 seats, it was the largest cultural complex of its kind. (The sixth theater, the 500-seat Terrace, opened in 1979.) Now, instead of avoiding Washington, world-class artists flocked to the capital city to perform in theaters that were perfectly sized to showcase their special talents.

The Center's formal opening was spectacular—a glittering two-day celebration (Opera House opening on September 8th and Concert Hall on the 9th) during which the high-ceilinged marble corridors were aswirl with elegantly dressed political and business leaders, artists, stage and film celebrities. Many of the by-invitation-only guests had donated tens, and even hundreds, of thousands of dollars to the Center.

Hundreds of tourists and celebrity-gawkers, attracted by the glamor, made a mob scene on the Plaza as frenzied as any Oscar night in Hollywood.

Inside, the Opera House glowed like a finely-polished gem. Its royal red carpeting and upholstery was striking beneath nearly 2,000 lights of a massive "starburst" crystal chandelier, a gift from Austria.

On opening night Rose Kennedy, the late President's mother, sat in the place of honor in the president's box. She was surrounded by many family members and friends including Leonard Bernstein, Mayor Walter Washington and Mr. and Mrs. Roger L. Stevens. Jacqueline Kennedy Onassis did not attend the gala opening, reportedly due to a last minute decision to avoid creating a mob scene. However, she wrote a moving tribute to the Center titled "A Dream Realized" which appeared in the September 1971 *Ladies' Home Journal*. Her tribute to the "gracious and serene" building rising on the banks of the Potomac acknowledged not only the high-profile Washingtonians behind the Center, but the hundreds of unknown artisans and construction workers who brought the dream to reality. And, striking to the core of the Center's mission, she declared that it "must not be a shrine, resplendent but lifeless . . . but a working place. . .alive with ideas and experiment . . . ."

In his opening comments that night, Roger Stevens saluted the man they were honoring with these words: "President Kennedy, more than any of his predecessors, lent dignity to the role of the arts in America . . . . We have tried to do justice to his memory."

The program on opening night of the Opera House

was as spirited and spectacular as the building itself—the premier performance of Leonard Bernstein's *Mass*, composed especially for the dedication at the request of Jacqueline Kennedy. A once-in-a-lifetime experience, *Mass* was described by *The Washington Post* music critic as "a rich amalgam of theatrical arts. . .a shattering experience." Isaac Stern called it the "best thing Bernstein's ever written."

It's easy to see why. A dramatic, theatrical pageant which used part of the liturgy of the Roman Mass, the production pulsated with a mix of languages and rhythms including Latin, slang, jazz and blues. Its sound surged from five musical groups. There were strings, organ and percussion in the pit. On stage were two rock bands, a brass marching band and a woodwind ensemble, plus some 200 dancers, choristers and soloists all costumed in brilliant, jewel-bright tones.

Bernstein said that he hoped the audience would be so moved by the *Mass* that instead of clapping, they'd "leap from their seats and embrace each other." Newspaper accounts don't mention if he got his wish though there are reports that some of the audience, emotionally overwhelmed, exchanged the Kiss of Peace as the last chords died away. Bernstein, himself, was so overcome during each of three performance nights that tears wet his cheeks and at times his body bowed over as if in prayer. At the end, he leapt about, bear-hugging and kissing everyone in sight, including the cast on stage.

The dedication of the Concert Hall the next night brought out an equally sparkling audience that included President and Mrs. Nixon who shared the presidential box with, among others, Mamie Eisenhower and Rose Kennedy. The National Symphony, directed by Antal Dorati, opened the program with Beethoven's *The Consecration of the House* which had also inaugurated the Josephstadt Theater in Vienna in 1823. The program also included Stravinsky's *Rite of Spring*, William Schuman's *A Free Song* and Mozart's *Violin Concerto in G* with Isaac Stern as soloist.

Although newspaper reports described the atmosphere as less rousing than the evening before (could anything ever compare with that highly charged event?), one special person was ebullient. Isaac Stern reportedly rhapsodized over the Hall's "fantastic" acoustics. "I had a ball! I used the hall like an instrument, just letting the sound out, letting it float!" he declared.

A month and a half later, actress Claire Bloom formally opened the intimate Eisenhower Theater with Ibsen's *A Doll's House*. It was the first of hundreds of productions that have included all kinds from Shakespeare to Lily Tomlin.

In the years since its opening, the Kennedy Center has presented more performing arts, in a broad range of talent, than any other single institution in the country. Some productions—new works or revivals of older ones—are produced or co-produced by the Center, which is responsible for both production and financing. Other times, the Center acts as a presenter of a company or an artist. In that case it assumes artistic and financial responsibility for the engagement. It receives revenues from ticket sales, but in turn it pays artists' fees, backstage salaries and the costs of marketing, advertising, and salaries of ushers and ticket office staff.

In recent years, the Center has enlarged its role as a commissioner of new works by Americans such as *Company B* which Paul Taylor created for the Houston Ballet. Additionally, the Center encourages and supports the work of new and innovative playwrights through its Fund for New American Plays, which is financed in conjunction with American Express and whose driving force is founding chairman Roger L. Stevens. Wendy Wasserstein's *The Heidi Chronicles*, Robert Schenkkan's six-hour-long *The Kentucky Cycle* and Tony Kushner's *Angels In America*, all Pulitzer Prize winners, owe much of their existence and success to grants and moral support from the Fund.

With the opening of the Center in that promising autumn of 1971, Washington at long last shed its reputation as a cultural desert. The front page of *The New York Times* said it all: "The capital of this nation finally strode into the cultural age tonight with the spectacular opening of the $70 million John F. Kennedy Center for the Performing Arts . . . a gigantic marble temple to music, dance and drama on the Potomac's edge."

In Washington, an editorial in the *Evening Star* assigned due credit for the Center's success. "In the face of criticism from every side, (Roger L.) Stevens persevered. To him more than anyone else we owe the glittering future the Center insures for the performing arts in our city, the capital of the nation."

Culture wasn't the only thing you could get at the new Center. As *Washington Post* writer Myra Mac-Pherson happily reported, the Center was the first theater in town where you could get an alcoholic drink at intermission. "A civilized European tradition," she declared.

Now, let's take a tour of that lovely, lively, marble temple on the Potomac.

2 A Sparkling Prelude

It's a typical lively evening at the Kennedy Center. At its two main entrances—the Hall of Nations and the Hall of States—taxis, busses, private cars and stretch limos jockey for position to deliver theater-goers, then glide swiftly away down the tree-lined plaza.

Programs in the six theaters tonight include a symphony benefit performance, an opening night of a rock musical, a comic murder mystery and an avant-garde drama. The audience's go-to-the-theater clothes reflect the mix. Black ties and evening gowns mingle with business suits, designer dresses, sweaters and skirts, jeans and T-shirts. Ballet is on the program too, which accounts for the dozens of small, budding ballerinas gaily hopping about in pastel party dresses.

Also weaving through the crowds in the marble-lined, red-carpeted halls are clusters of foot-weary tourists, doggedly following the upraised umbrellas used by commercial tour guides to keep themselves in sight of their group, and trying simultaneously to spot their state flags amid the bright banners that hang high above in the Hall of States. The flags represent all 50 states, the District of Columbia and the five territories of Puerto Rico, the Virgin Islands, Guam, American Samoa and the Commonwealth of North Mariana Islands.

If you know your state history, you can find your flag in a flash because they're hung in the order in which the states entered the union, beginning on the right as you face the plaza entrance. In the Hall of Nations, hung with flags of countries where the United States has diplomatic missions, the order is alphabetical. When a country changes its name, work crews hop into a telescoping scaffold and rise 60 feet in the air to rearrange the flags.

Whether you enter the Center through the Hall of

States or the parallel Hall of Nations, eventually you'll come to the Grand Foyer, the vast hall that runs the length of the building on its river side. The foyer, which serves as the lobby for the Center's three main theaters, is one of the biggest rooms in the world. With its gift shop, main box office and information desk, the Hall of States is the busier of the two halls. Here, too, tucked into the corner near the entrance, is the 224-seat American Film Institute (AFI) Theater, a gift from Jack L. Warner of Warner Brothers, to showcase the finest films from around the world. There are more than 700 screenings every year. This isn't a theater for popcorn eaters and chatterboxes. In fact, noisy popcorn is taboo. These patrons view film as an art form, and they enjoy it in a setting that has great sightlines from every seat and the finest sound equipment. The decor is a spare but imaginative design of exposed scaffolding and grey concrete block walls on which are hung several blue, spray-painted automobile hoods. Each night, in this "backstage" atmosphere, die-hard movie buffs watch, analyze and enjoy new releases as well as grand old classics. The theater is occasionally rented by large corporations for symposia. However, anyone may invite friends and treat them to an "evening-at-the-movies" with showings of the best of the old silent films complete with live organ accompaniment.

But the AFI is far more than a movie theater. It's a non-profit organization, set up in 1967, to preserve the heritage of film and television and to train new talent in the wide, varied world of "moving images." At its Center for Advance Film and Television Studies on its Los Angeles campus, the AFI offers specialized training in producing, directing, screenwriting, cinematography, editing and production design. The Institute is also responsible for acquiring films for preservation which it transfers to the Library of Congress and 18 other archives around the world. To date, this collection program, funded by the National Endowment for the Arts, has acquired more than 25,000 films.

In the Halls of States and Nations soft spotlights on the marble-clad walls make a lustrous sheen and the buffed floors shine like ice under a sheet of water.

The marble is the finest quality stone from Carrara, the marble of Michelangelo. To honor President Kennedy the Italians sent 3,700 tons of marble to sheath the Center, inside and out. Each stone block, cut to fit an exact spot on the Center's walls, was numbered and labeled in Italy. "Marble is durable, but even more durable is friendship," said the Italian Ambassador when he presented the gift. As its contribution to the memorial, The American Shipping Lines donated the cost of bringing the marble to the United States.

In the stairwell from the Hall of States to the lower level is Brazil's gift to the Center, a large, deeply textured wool fiber artwork in earthy tones reminiscent of adobe brick, clay and maize. Titled *Caroa*, meaning "crown," it's the work of Brazilian artist Jacques Douchez.

Complementing *Caroa* in the stairwell of the Hall of Nations is Peru's gift, a haunting oil painting of shadowy, half-seen faces, melting spheres, blurred lights and a peaceful sea of cerulean blue. It's titled *Transfiguration*, and is the work of Peruvian painter Antonio Maro.

At night when the Center's lights are blazing, it's a breathtaking moment when theater-goers walk between the slim, gilded pillars at the entrance of the Grand Foyer from the Halls of States and Nations. Like those two great halls, the foyer, which is 60 feet high, 40 feet wide and 630 feet long, is carpeted in rich, royal red. The carpet is a large part of the building's total 19,000 square yards of red carpet. Imagine flipping the Washington Monument onto its side and placing it in the Grand Foyer. It fits—with 75 feet left over! Or, you could put two football fields in the foyer and have ten yards to spare.

The foyer's 60-foot high, double-paned, acoustical windows, set in cream-colored walls, overlook the river terrace. They're hung with gold metallic-weave draperies. In the middle of the foyer, flanking the entrance to the Opera House, is the gift from Belgium, eight dramatic panels of world-famous Belgian mirror, each one nine feet wide and 58 feet high. Smaller panels decorate the Box Tier.

Overhead, running the length of the hall, are 18

High-hung flags of more than 160 countries lend a heraldic note to the long, marble-lined Hall of Nations.

In an open-air studio under clear Italian skies in Pietrasanta, using a 15-inch head as a model, Robert Berks works on his 8-foot, monumental bust of President Kennedy.

glittering Orrefors crystal chandeliers which one awe-struck young lady likened to diamond-drop earrings—"earrings" that are 15 feet long, seven feet across and weigh a ton each. The chandeliers and matching wall sconces are Sweden's gift to the Center.

Each chandelier has 64 hexagonal units with 12, hand-blown double prisms of lead crystal and six lights. Twenty-two wall sconces add another 176 units. That's nearly 8,000 lights shining through 16,000 double prisms, breathtakingly reflected in the 60-foot high mirrors and glass doors.

The color of the chandeliers' light varies with the seasons and time of day. On dark winter nights, the glow is warm and golden; in summer when the late afternoon sun strikes the crystal, it creates countless exploding splinters of crystalline light—almost too bright to look at without squinting.

Outside, on the tree-dotted terrace, underwater lighting adds blue-white sparkle to splashing fountains. Garden greenery surrounds the Center, including weeping willows and a thick carpet of ivy which has grown from 13,000 English ivy plants, a gift-that-keeps-on-growing from the American Association of Nurserymen. On pleasant evenings, theater-goers stroll on the terrace, nibbling snacks purchased from colorful, canopied food carts and taking in the view of the Potomac. Yachts, sailboats and sculls dot the river. Theodore Roosevelt Island, an 88-acre wilderness preserve, is visible just across from the Center.

Amid such splendor, it's not surprising when a little girl in a fancy dress and lace-trimmed socks confides to her mom that someday she'd like to get married here.

The focal point of the Grand Foyer is the dramatically spotlighted, eight-foot high bronze bust of President Kennedy. The 3,000-pound bust, which rests on a slim ten-foot pedestal of beige travertine, was done by American sculptor Robert Berks whom *The New York Times* has called Washington's Michelangelo. His many public monuments of famous people include the figure of Albert Einstein on the lawn of the National Academy of Sciences in Washington. Einstein looks so inviting that children climb into his lap.

The story behind the sculpture began the night that President Kennedy was assassinated. In his sorrow, Robert Berks was moved to action. "I felt I had to do something," he says. "Out of 800 pictures that I had of the President, I chose 80, spread them out on the floor, climbed a 12-foot high ladder, studied them for three hours, and then and there created a half life-size bust in clay—a special clay of mine that looks like bronze so I can see how the finished piece will look when light strikes it."

That small bust, plus another "heroic head"—one and a half times life-size—came to the attention of the Kennedy family via numerous people in the art world and ultimately led to the commission of the bust for the new memorial.

"I felt deeply committed to the mission and was conscious of two goals," Mr. Berks explains. "First, to capture the whole Kennedy spirit of encouraging creative arts. Secondly, I was keenly aware that this was to be the only monument to President Kennedy in Washington, and that I was responsible for creating an image for the centuries. That's the kind of work I do— for the ages, not a mere hundred years." He pauses.

"You might call me a 'centurist' sculptor," he adds.

Mr. Berks is also a "method sculptor," becoming one with his subjects just as method actors meld with their characters. In the case of President Kennedy, Mr. Berks was inspired by the "young hero" spirit of the young president and the hopefulness that he gave the country. To convey this vitality and the president's multi-faceted personality, Mr. Berks employed the craggy, rough-textured surface that causes so much comment when people see it for the first time. As viewers move around the bust and look at it in different lights, as the sculptor intended, they can glimpse the variety of expressions of the president's character—his youth, athleticism, statesmanship, and even his vulnerability.

The total design of the bust, including placement and lighting, took Mr. Berks nearly six years. One of the first problems was to figure out what size bust would be right for the Grand Foyer. He solved the problem by trial and error. Next to his home in Long Island, New York, he marked off an area as big as the Grand Foyer in a 1,000-foot open field, an old potato field bordered by maple trees set 60 feet apart. He then painted 6-, 8- and 10-foot high heads of President Kennedy and placed them in the field. He studied and measured until he knew exactly what he needed—an eight-foot figure. "It had to be big enough so it wouldn't get lost in that huge space. It had to be the host of the foyer," he explains.

"The size and placement of the bust, in effect, reduce the scale of the Grand Foyer. You get the feeling that you and the president are totally alone. He fills the place. He is the life force of the whole Center." Mr. Berks adds that a bust this size would not have been acceptable before the invention of cinema which has made it commonplace to see faces magnified to 20 feet high and wide.

To manufacture the bust, Mr. Berks went to Pietrasanta, Italy, near Carrara where Michelangelo discovered a mother-lode of fine white marble. Even now, 500 years later, the region is still renowned for its exceptionally fine stone quarries, as well as the masons and foundrymen needed for the bronze casting.

Despite the fact that casting rough texture is very difficult, the bust was made and cast in an incredibly short five months to meet the deadline of the opening of the Center. Mr. Berks worked outdoors in the Italian mountains in the company of other sculptors, assistants and apprentices in a "wonderful atmosphere" reminiscent of the open-air sculpture studios of Michelangelo's day.

The trip to Washington with the huge bust was far less romantic and fascinating. In fact, it was hair-raising and heart-stopping. Crated and hauled to the American air base in Pisa, the bust was fork-lifted onto an old DC8 called the *Red Baron* that still had bullet holes in it from past service in the Pakistani Air Force. As Mr. Berks recalls, "The seats had been taken out, lots of mail bags and stuff were strewn about. There was only myself, the pilot, co-pilot and a combined navigator-engineer. I was given some stale sandwiches that had been made the day before in Germany and a parachute. 'If anything goes wrong, jump!' they said."

Something did go wrong. Half-way across the Atlantic, at the point of no return, the engineer announced that the emergency oxygen supply was gone. They flew the rest of the way to Gander, Newfoundland, at 12,000 feet through "really bumpy weather."

More bad luck. The malfunctioning equipment couldn't be replaced or repaired. The flight had to continue south to Washington at 9,000 feet–straight through thunderstorms. Blue light (St. Elmo's Fire) danced around the nose of the plane, and bolts of lightning shot through it—once, twice, three times. Each time it "literally pounded my chest," Mr. Berks recalls. "I was never so scared in my life!"

What about the bust? Was he horror-stricken that it might be damaged or destroyed? "Not really," he says matter-of-factly. "When I'm deeply emotionally involved with something, I have utter faith that all will go well. I had the very deep feeling that the bust would get to its proper place. You see, I have a guardian angel who gets me through every circumstance. He does fool around a lot in the process, though," he adds with a chuckle.

Naturally there was great curiosity about this huge

bust that was to dominate the Grand Foyer, especially when President Nixon decreed that there was to be no advance information or pictures. But one picture did leak—a photo that an AP photographer managed to get while the bust was in the open-air studio in Italy. And so, the secrecy was broken, and the first photo of the bust was flashed around the world—President Kennedy in bronze being given a final polishing by the sculptor dressed in his work shorts!

Working with "lighting genius" Abe Feder, Mr. Berks designed the special ceiling spotlights which throw two beams of light onto the bust, one cool and one warm and angled so that their beams don't clash with the crystal chandeliers.

There's a practical footnote to the story. Because people tend to look at a bust head-on, the sculpture could not be placed so as to face the Opera House squarely; if it had been, people coming out of the theater would stop to look and cause traffic jams. Mr. Berks accounted for that by angling the bust so that the president gazes nine feet to the right of center. People unconsciously step out of the main traffic flow to look at it.

In the late afternoon pause between matinee and evening performances, the Grand Foyer is dramatic—slashed by stripes of sun and shadow.

Glittering and elegant as it is, the Grand Foyer can also be cheerful and welcoming. Often it's casual and downright homey, thanks to many, mostly free, activities: balalaika bands, Irish jig dancers, Japanese drummers, even minuet dancers from the Mozart Festival in 18th-century costumes. Most weeks, there are noon-time concerts by young musicians from Washington area high schools and colleges. It's a delightfully informal scene with the musicians grouped under the Kennedy bust and the audience sprawled on the Opera House steps, munching on brown-bag lunches.

At Christmas, the Grand Foyer, decorated with dozens of white-lighted fir trees, is the scene of continual festivals of choirs, chamber music groups and handbell ringers, culminating with Viennese waltzes beneath the crystal chandeliers on New Year's Eve.

But now, the light of the chandeliers begins to flicker, signaling curtain time. Quickly, the audiences file into the theaters, and until intermission, the Grand Foyer sparkles quietly on its own.

3 | *The Sounds of Music*

On a cool spring evening in 1993, soprano Jessye Norman, resplendent in a golden gown, held her Concert Hall audience rapt with her incomparable singing of "He's Got The Whole World In His Hands."

So superb are the Concert Hall's acoustics that every one of Ms. Norman's notes, even the softest, rose true and clear to every corner of the 2,750-seat hall, the largest in the Kennedy Center.

The design that made this flawless sound possible is the incredible work of the Center's acoustical designer, Dr. Cyril Harris, currently Professor Emeritus, Department of Electrical Engineering and the School of Architecture, Columbia University. Dr. Harris made use of almost every physical feature of the great hall to reflect and diffuse sounds as perfectly as possible.

Ranks of gleaming organ pipes (4,187 of them) crown the huge stage of the 2,750 seat Concert Hall.

But before considering the beautiful sounds inside the six theaters, consider the not-so-melodious noises that must be kept out. Visitors are always curious about how the theaters are sound-proofed against jet plane noise from near-by National Airport. Planes continuously take off in a steep, roaring climb over the Center. The aircraft noise may be the most noticeable, but it's only one of many unwanted sounds that assault the theaters. There's almost steady traffic noise from a busy highway that runs directly beneath the building's overhanging plaza on the Potomac River side. Add to that the murmuring buzz of thousands of people in the halls and Grand Foyer during intermissions, plus the vibration and humming of machinery in the kitchens and mechanical equipment rooms. The result is a virtual bombardment of noise. Some is carried through the air, and some is carried by vibration through the Center's skeleton and skin of metal, stone and wood.

The acoustical design of the Center is extremely

complex and technical, and can only be touched on here. One of its most intriguing aspects, a major element in noise control, lies in Dr. Harris' ingenious box-within-a-box construction design. Imagine each of the theaters as a small box with its own completely independent supporting columns enclosed within the large box of the Center.

A second important feature is Dr. Harris' use of double wall construction, each wall being made of 6-inch solid high-density concrete blocks separated by a 2-inch airspace filled with a fiber-glass blanket. When a plane flies low over the Center you may have to shout or halt conversation altogether on the outside river terrace, but in the theaters, cradled securely in their boxes, not a peep of aircraft noise gets through.

The sound and vibration of the Center's massive machinery has been eliminated inside the theaters by floating slab construction and resilient mounts among other acoustical design features. Potentially noisy pipes are fitted with flexible rather than rigid connectors. In the noise-reducing, double-window construction in the Grand Foyer, there are four inches of space between the half-inch thick interior panes of glass and the quarter-inch thick exterior panes. To further reduce vibration noise, the glass is mounted in resilient seals so there's no solid connection between the panes and their framework. As added noise control insurance, the theaters are encircled by what appears to be ordinary, carpeted passageways but, in fact, are carefully engineered "sound locks." Dr. Harris designed them just in case a theater patron opens a door to leave or enter the auditorium at the very moment a plane is flying by. The sound locks, with their acoustically-treated ceilings, special carpeting and sound-absorptive wall treatment, insure that the music and singing stay in the theaters and the aircraft noise stays out.

Now, away from unwanted sound, or noise, and back to the beautiful sounds of orchestras, choirs, soloists and actors—sounds that must be heard at their very best.

Because Dr. Harris worked with the architect, Edward Durrell Stone, in the early planning stages, he was able to recommend the best shape for the theaters

A bird's-eye view of the Concert Hall's coffered, hexagonal-design ceiling, light spheres and the inverted pyramids of Norwegian crystal chandeliers—all part of the hall's excellent acoustics system.

Musical instruments of biblical times, carved deeply in African walnut by Nechemia Azaz, create a joyful and dynamic wall in the Israeli Lounge. At the center, ringing words of the 150th Psalm sing praises with trumpets, harps and cymbals.

as well as the construction materials and design details that would result in the most desirable acoustics. This includes the solid wood that surrounds the orchestra, wood-over-plaster walls, overlapping wall panels, acoustical panels on the box tiers, 292 small decorative spheres on the ceiling and a foot-deep coffered ceiling in a pattern of hexagonal units each of which has stepped surfaces of slightly different sizes. Even the 11 Hadelands crystal chandeliers, (10 feet wide by 13 feet high) a gift from Norway, are part of the ingenious sound system. The hall's wooden floor, in Dr. Harris' words, "lets you literally feel the music through your feet." No wonder music critics have praised the hall as "acoustically flawless," "a modern miracle,"—and just plain "terrific!" (An insider's tip and professional opinion from Leo Gallenstein, Supervisor of Theater Operations in the Maintenance Department and repository of 45 years of fascinating theater lore: for sound, the best seats are in the last row of the center section of the second balcony.)

According to Dr. Harris, in a truly great music hall the audience feels totally immersed in sound, as if the music were coming at them from all directions—which, in fact, it is. The sounds bounce around the room, from pillar to post, ricocheting like pin-balls off all of those indentations, curves, nooks and crannies in the walls and ceiling. In the grand old 19th century halls in Europe, the ornate carvings, friezes, ornamental plastering, niches, cornices, statues, busts and extravaganzas of little winged cherubs weren't just gloriously romantic. They were also excellent sound diffusers. In today's clean-lined halls, the indentations of overlapping wall panels and the stepped surfaces of a coffered ceiling have replaced the romantic little cherubs. A point of interest: people's heads are also good diffusers, so a concert sounds better when it's sold out!

While heads and cherubs make good sound diffusers in music halls, clothing and carpets are negative forces because they absorb sound. Look at the special carpet in the Concert Hall. After extensive tests to find a carpet with low sound absorptive characteristics, Dr. Harris decided on a wool and nylon carpet with a pile height of .16 inches. It was laid directly on the concrete of the aisles and sound lock of the Concert Hall (leaving the wooden floor beneath the seats bare so music lovers can "listen" with their feet). The carpet is red. So is the carpet in the Grand Foyer and halls. But the likeness ends there. The hallway carpets are a heavier weight wool with a pile height of .5 inches, laid on padding. This heavier, thicker, highly absorptive carpet keeps the Grand Foyer as din-free as possible by drinking in the sounds of conversation and the clinking of ice cubes in cocktail glasses. Incidentally, because clothing absorbs sound, Dr. Harris recommends that audiences do their ears a favor by checking their coats in the cloakroom.

An acoustical test of the Concert Hall was the playing of Beethoven's Overture, *Leonore No. 3*, so it's fitting that the portrait of Beethoven was the first painting to hang in the stairwell of the Concert Hall. Its companion portrait of Haydn is in the opposite stairwell.

A true treasure of the Concert Hall is the magnificent Skinner Aeolian organ, whose 4,187 pipes form a majestic backdrop for the wide stage. Ranging from three-eighths of an inch to thirty-two feet high and one-and-a-half feet in diameter, the graduated ranks of burnished pipes might easily be imagined as the silvery, golden and copper spires of a grand, futuristic city. Or, equally imaginatively, as music critic Law-rence Sears commented in the *Washington Evening Star*, the pipes' "dramatic arrangement seems like a vast chord, frozen in majestic silence."

Unlike many organs that have non-working pipes strictly for show, this organ gets 100% work from each pipe. With no mock cylinders to deflect the fantastic sound, it bursts forth at full throttle, swelling to a fullness that's literally breathtaking and pulse-pounding.

This "Cadillac of organs"—so-called by its proud installer and curator, Mr. Irving Lawless—was given to the Center by Mrs. Kay Shouse in memory of her parents, Mr. and Mrs. Lincoln Filene. It was dedicated in February 1972 with a specially commissioned work by John La Montaine, *Wilderness Journal*. Based on the writings of Thoreau, the piece was written for organ, orchestra and baritone. The performers that evening were the National Symphony Orchestra, Paul Callaway on organ and Donald Graham, soloist. Today, from time to time the organ plays in concert with the National Symphony, but its really big workout comes during the Christmas holidays.

Not surprisingly, the elegant Concert Hall is popular for high school graduations, and every spring the magnificent organ pours out stirring, lump-in-the-throat processional music for capped-and-gowned young men and women.

Apart from the organ pipes that crown it, the Concert Hall stage itself is a barren expanse of wood and not particularly exceptional—until you think of the thousands of young musicians who had a hand in building it, not with hammer and nails, but with their music. For, all across the United States, Canada, England and Japan, 692 school and community orchestras and bands gave benefit concerts to raise the money to build the splendid, solid wood stage. Dedicated to John Philip Sousa, the stage can hold two hundred people.

The Concert Hall is the home of the National Symphony Orchestra but that doesn't mean that music there is limited to the classics. Jazz, blues, rock, bluegrass, folk songs and dances—you name it and it's been heard or seen here, along with rhythmic clapping

Four-year-old Sam finds new ways to look at—and through— Figure *by Great Britain's Dame Barbara Hepworth.*

and dancing in the aisles!

Like the Opera House and Eisenhower Theater, the Concert Hall has a President's Box in the middle of the first balcony. When the president comes to the theater, the seal of the United States is hung on the front of his box, so the audience knows he's there—as if they weren't aware of that the minute they enter the building and have to pass through super-tight security screening! All handbags are scrutinized, even those of celebrities.

The seats in the president's boxes are the only seats in the Center that aren't for sale to the general public. When the president isn't using his box, the White House determines its use by White House staff, government officials or visiting dignitaries. It's a popular prestige symbol for not only are the seats the best in the house, but there's a small private lounge just behind the box complete with a little refrigerator which the White House keeps stocked with soft drinks and souvenir bottles of champagne bearing the presidential seal. Also stamped with the presidential seal are M&M's chocolate candies.

Traditionally, each incoming president decorates the small lounge with pictures. The Bushes hung informal shots of the president playing tennis and Barbara Bush playing with First Dog Millie on the White House lawn. The Clinton photos show a serious president taking his oath of office and a romantic president and first lady dancing cheek to cheek at an inaugural ball. There is a lovely, relaxed mother-daughter photo of Hillary and Chelsea Clinton in their inaugural gowns.

Scattered through the Center are numerous handsome lounges used for receptions, press conferences, board meetings, cocktail parties and the like. Each one has a distinctive decor and ambiance. The Israeli Lounge, adjacent to the Concert Hall, for example, is decorated with paintings and carvings that have bright, joyous musical themes. In this lounge, which was a gift of the people of Israel, you're literally surrounded by art, for three of Israel's finest artists have carved and painted the walls and the ceiling with scenes of Biblical stories.

The entire wall to the left as you enter is paneled

with African walnut wood and covered with nearly three-dimensional carvings of ancient musical instruments mentioned in the Bible. The work of Nechemia Asaz, they're highlighted with brass and copper. Words from the 150th Psalm are carved in the center of the wall.

The other three walls are equally unique. They are covered with cream-colored nylon and silk panels on which abstract artist Yehezkil Kimchi has sketched the history of Israel in sepia ink. On one panel the hand of God is extended from heaven toward His people.

Artist Shraga Weil has splashed the ceiling with brilliantly colored paints and 22-carat gold leaf with more scenes from the Old Testament. David strums his harp, Miriam dances triumphantly to celebrate the passage of the Israelites through the Red Sea, and a choir of boys raise their voices in song on the temple steps.

On the doorpost of the lounge you will see a traditional mezuzah, a tubular case holding a rolled up bit of parchment with verses from the book of Deuteronomy that ask for a blessing on the room.

Just outside the lounge is Sir Jacob Epstein's bronze bust of Hans Kindler who was the founder and first music director of the National Symphony Orchestra. The bust was made in the late 1920s when the sculptor and the maestro were good friends in London.

Every year thousands of school children descend on the Kennedy Center by the busload to attend free concerts, ballets, plays, story-telling hours, and, of course, to take tours. It's all part of the Center's education program to help children develop an eye and appreciation for the arts. Some already have a fantastic "eye," for art. They view things in delightfully imaginative ways. For example, Luxembourg's gift to the Center, located just outside of the Israeli Lounge, is a highly polished, pale pink marble sculpture called *Ascension* which conveys an upward reaching of the spirit. An imaginative fourth-grade boy, studying it intently, finally declared that it looks like "fat music notes carved out of strawberry ice cream." One hopes that Lucien Wercollier, the sculptor, would credit him for an unusually creative interpretation.

Two other boys had equally creative ways of looking

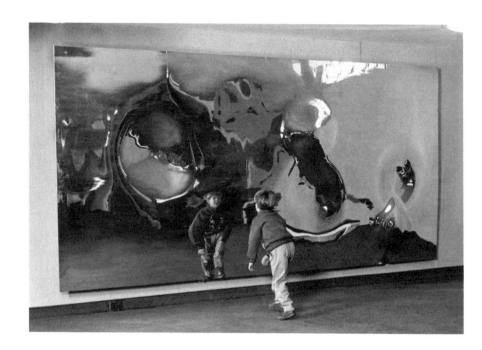

at the gift from Great Britain, the six-foot tall abstract bronze sculpture called *Figure* by Dame Barbara Hepworth. While the adults admired the bronze's subtle and incomparable sculpting and shading, one youngster leaned over, gazed at it sideways and announced that its oval openings were "just like the Lone Ranger's mask." Another, maybe a budding musician, called it a "giant kazoo." Clearly, it's a sculpture for all ages.

In vivid contrast to the smooth-lined *Figure* is the nearby bust of Dmitri Shostakovich. Deeply and expressively modeled, it was a gift from cellist and longtime National Symphony Orchestra director Mstislav Rostropovich to commemorate the 70th birthday of his friend, the composer. (Though there is no official gift to the Center from the former U.S.S.R.—those were *pre-glasnost days*—many people like to think of Maestro Rostropovich as the Center's gift from Russia.)

On the orchestra level, two large wall sculptures balance one another at opposite ends of the entry to the Concert Hall. On one side is a creamy-white, deeply cut, unglazed porcelain relief called *Vibrations* done in five sections, each 69 inches high and 30 inches wide, within a stainless steel frame. The gift of the people of Denmark, it was made in the Royal Porcelain Factory by sculptress Inge-Lise Koefed and traveled in first class style on the Royal Danish yacht with Queen Margrethe II when she visited the United States during the Bicentennial celebration. The artist intends her work to express the movements and tensions between human beings and nature by what she calls "white graphics" in which light casts shadows of varying depths and widths on the carved clay.

Opposite *Vibrations* is the gift of Switzerland, a favorite with youngsters because it practically shouts, "Hey, art can be fun!" Kids' eyes widen when they learn how artist Willy Weber made this wall sculpture—by exploding dynamite on both sides of a 500-pound sheet of steel to create irregularly shaped curves, craters and bumps. After chrome-plating the steel and polishing it to a mirror-like finish, Weber christened it *Apollo X 1970*. Most viewers see it as a strange and wonderful moonscape although that wasn't the artist's intent.

Kids find it strange and wonderful, like a fun house mirror. The shiny convex/concave surface elongates and contorts their images as they make faces and, giggling, bend and twist in front of it. Weber would probably love to watch their antics because he intended the piece to be looked at imaginatively and creatively, to come to life by reflecting figures and light playing on it. He wants the viewer to participate in its creation. Teen-agers invariably "participate" by cooly touching up their hair. It's hard to beat the interpretations of a group of nine-year olds who saw the shapes on Apollo's undulating surface as balloons, seashells and "curves like the Phantom's mask." But imagine, if you will, a line-up of charming 10-year-old ballet students pirouetting solemnly in front of *Apollo X* suddenly catching a look at their bizarre moonscape reflections and bursting into gales of giggles.

When the National Symphony Orchestra practices in the Concert Hall, the music floats through loudspeakers into the entry way, a delightful background for viewing—or pirouetting in front of—the art.

Next stop on the tour, the Opera House.

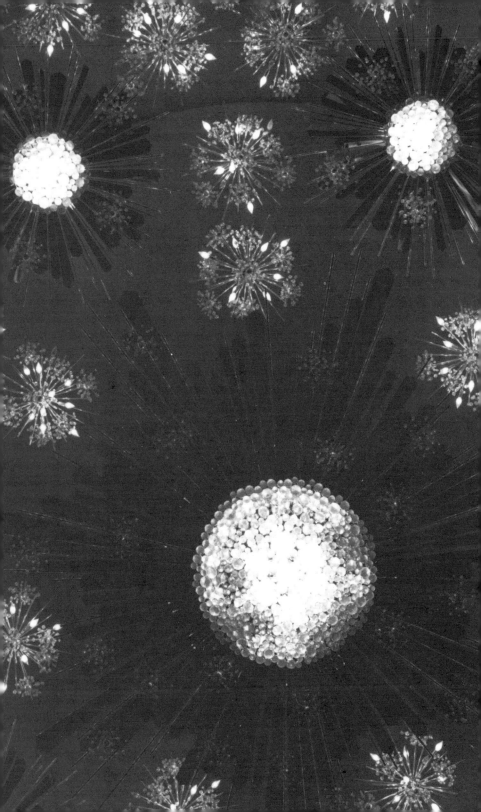

4 Curtain Up!

Red is the color of drama. Appropriately, red *is* the Kennedy Center Opera House—walls, floors, curtain, and even ceiling. The perfect color for a theater where heros clash swords with villains, and sopranos, rapturously singing, sink to their deaths.

Equally dramatic is the lighting that gives the red its rich glow—a 50-foot wide chandelier in the design of a brilliant, multi-rayed sun bursting into a galaxy of glittering lights.

The spectacular chandelier, a gift from Austria, is made of Lobmeyr crystal. It's set into the high dome of the Opera House and has 1,735 light bulbs. Cleaning the chandelier and changing burnt-out bulbs, or relamping, is done every three years by a stagehand who isn't afraid of heights. He climbs into the bucket of a very long-armed cherry picker and is raised to the ceiling. In addition to replacing bulbs, he removes clusters of crystals from the chandelier, brings them down to floor level where they are washed in water and detergent, dried and polished before being taken back up in the bucket, once again to sparkle overhead.

Starburst? Snowflakes? Fireworks? The Austrian crystal chandelier that blazes across the ceiling of the Opera House sparkles with the light of 1,735 bulbs.

One of the loveliest sights in the Kennedy Center is the dimming of the Opera House chandelier in the moments before the curtain goes up. Its clear, sparkling light gradually softens to tones of peach, then glowing apricot and deep copper and finally darkness.

The Kennedy Center is the home of the highly regarded Washington Opera, the seventh largest company in the country, which plays in the Opera House to standing room only. But the name "Opera House" shouldn't mislead you. The theater, with its 100 x 68 foot stage, big orchestra pit (large enough for 100 musicians) and its top-notch acoustics ("Not a dead spot in the house," says theater manager Richard Kidwell), is also perfect for star-studded Broadway musicals, dramas and world-class ballet companies. Over the years, the Opera House stage has echoed with the footsteps and voices of dancers and singers from companies such as the New York City Ballet, American Ballet Theater, The Stuttgart, Bolshoi, Kirov and Royal Ballets, Paris Opera Ballet, Royal Danish Ballet, Dance Theater of Harlem, Grand Kabuki of Japan, Deutsche Oper Berlin, Vienna State Opera and La Scala. Some productions include *Chorus Line, Phantom of the Opera, Guys and Dolls* and *Les Miserables*, to name just a few. Backstage, Rehearsal Hall #1 is large enough to lay out a full stage for rehearsals of productions this size.

When the Bolshoi Ballet traveled from Moscow to perform at the Center, its "luggage" was carried by 54 tractor trailers. It took 100 stagehands working in shifts around the clock two weeks to unload the road boxes. Even those who didn't speak Russian learned quickly that "bolshoi" means "big." The Opera House was up to the task of stowing every bit of scenery and lights, sound equipment and costumes that the Bolshoi brought with them.

The elegant curtain that rises on these big, exciting productions is (what else?) red—red silk patterned with gold, a gift from Japan. A big gift, 47 by 117 feet and weighing 3,000 pounds, its size created a problem. It was too big to be woven by hand, yet it needed the sensitivity of hand weaving to convey the feeling of rhythm in the gentle curves of its design.

The ingenious solution of Kyoto's master weavers was to combine mechanical and hand work, for which they had to build a special Jacquard weaving machine, the world's largest, with 3,600 needles. The rhythmic pattern of the curtain is called *Springing Flowers*, a Japanese symbol of progress in honor of the frontier spirit of President Kennedy. Behind this poetic curtain hangs the practical one, a 7,000-pound fire curtain that cuts off the backstage area from the 2,350 theater seats in the event of fire.

A very special event, the Kennedy Center Honors Gala, takes place in the Opera House every December. It's a glittering evening of tribute to five or six of the country's most productive, creative and distinguished artists who have made invaluable contributions to the country's cultural life. Adorned with medals on rainbow colored ribbons, they join the President and his wife in his box to enjoy lavish stage entertainment in their honor. Over the years, since the inception of the honors gala in 1978, honorees have included artists as diverse as Lena Horne, Danny Kaye, Isaac Stern, Beverly Sills, Perry Como, Sammy Davis Jr., Alvin Ailey, George Burns, Harry Belafonte, Tennessee Williams, Leontyne Price and Fred Astaire. More recent honorees are Ginger Rogers, Paul Newman and Joanne Woodward, choreographer Paul Taylor, Lionel Hampton, Maestro Mstislav Rostropovich, choreographer and Dance Theater of Harlem founder Arthur Mitchell, Maestro Georg Solti, Johnny Carson, Stephen Sondheim and gospel singer Marion Williams.

The gala is taped and shown on CBS stations nationwide later in the month. Incidentally, because the orchestra is on stage instead of in the pit for the Honors Gala, it's one of the rare occasions on which the stage is extended to its fullest by removing the first six rows of seats and raising the floor to stage level. It has also been extended for Shakespeare readings to bring the actors closer to the audience. When the Vienna State Opera performed on stage, the floor of the orchestra pit was raised part way so that the musicians' heads could be seen by the audience and singers, as they are in Vienna.

Another movable floor is the special one laid on the stage for ballet performances. It consists of two layers of wood with an inch or two of space between them to give dancers a "springy" foundation that's easier on their joints than a floor based on steel and concrete. When not in use the floor is stored, in sections, below the stage.

The middle door leading into the Opera House from the lobby is flanked by two opulently dressed sentinels encased in glass. These are mannequins dressed in costumes from recent Washington Opera productions. The costumes are changed periodically to give theatergoers a close look at the detailed workmanship and lavish materials–silks, satins, velvets, reams of lace and heaps of seed-pearls—that go into the productions. The costumes, valued at an average of $4,000 each,

Effortlessly, fluidly, Matisse's Fish of the Sea *leap and glide across a tapestry palette of white, creams, greys and blues.*

are so well constructed that they give about 20 years of good service to the Washington Opera and other companies who rent productions from the "WashOp."

The right and left stairwells leading from the main floor to the box tier of the Opera House are enlivened by a pair of large abstract oil paintings that are one of two gifts from Argentina. (The other gift, a bronze sculpture titled *Phoenix* by Libero Badii, stands on the first tier of the Concert Hall.) The paintings, by the well-known Argentine artist Raquel Forner, are dynamic in color, texture and name—*Combat of Astrobeings*. Part of the artist's series of "Space" paintings, they show an imaginary struggle between beings of a star world. Vivid splashes of red on the canvas (blood on the battlefield?) echo the bright color of the carpet. Kids love the idea of Astro-beings locked in bloody battle, and the paintings are terrific imagination-igniters for the hundreds of youngsters whose tours of the Center introduce them to a variety of art.

At the top of one stairwell is another lively work of art, a bronze plaque of Julius Rudel, the Center's first music director, who seems to lean out of the bronze, baton in hand, in the energetic pose of a maestro. Commissioned by the Kennedy Center, the relief was sculpted by Una Hanbury.

"I know who did those!" an excited nine-year old boy exclaimed to a tour guide who was pointing to the tapestries that are a gift of France. "It's the same guy who cut out all those paper patterns that we saw at the art museum," he announced.

The youngster knew his art. The "guy" was French artist Henri Matisse, who, besides cutting out museum-quality paper patterns, designed two striking blue and white tapestries, woven at the Gobelin Factory in Paris, that hang at either end of the Opera House's box tier. Titled *Birds of the Air* and *Fish of the Sea*, the 6 x 10 feet hangings feature the seemingly simple shapes that are the signature of Matisse's work, the signature that the nine-year old proudly spotted.

Several bronzes ornament the box tier. One, a bust of Senator J. William Fulbright, created by Gretta Bader, honors the senator for his deep involvement with the Center, first as the man who introduced the original legislation for a national culture center and, later, as an active member of the Board.

Flanking the row of entrances to the box seats are two more gifts from France, bronze figures by French sculptor Henri Laurens. One, a supine figure called *Autumn* might well be lolling beneath a tree, admiring its colorful canopy. The other, *Ocean Nymph*, is a lush figure who seems to ride the crest of waves. Her big toe has been worn shiny by theater-goers who touch it as they pass, possibly for good luck.

Another bronze figure, the gift of Greece, dominates the center of the box tier. It's Poseidon, the ancient Greek god of the sea. At six-foot, ten inches and 265 pounds, the muscular god seems to burst with energy. He has taken a strong stance with arm upraised as if to hurl his trident. Except that there's no trident there.

There is a story behind the missing spear. Back in about 460 B.C. an ancient Greek sculptor cast a bronze statue of Poseidon holding his trident. Somehow it was lost in a shipwreck and not found for centuries until, in 1926, some Greek fishermen in the Mediterranean "caught" part of the statue in their nets. Two years later, the Greek Archeological Service found all the rest except for the trident. Poseidon is one of the most important surviving Greek works of art. The original

Bold and heroic, the 6'10" bronze figure of Poseidon, god of the sea, dominates the box tier of the Opera House.

stands in an Athens museum. The Kennedy Center's statue is an exact bronze cast, which accounts for the missing three-pronged spear. Tour guides hear a lot of comments at this statue because, of course, Poseidon is a classical nude. As youngsters giggle-whisper, "He's naked!"

The two lounges on the box tier of the Opera House, the African Lounge and the South Opera Lounge, are as different in style and ambiance as two

In the African Lounge the atmosphere of a typical African village is symbolized by tribal cloth hangings, dramatically slanted and textured walls and floating ceiling panels.

rooms can be, one hushed and solemn, the other crying out to be the setting of a sparkling champagne reception.

From the moment you step into the quiet African Lounge, a reception room for dignitaries, you sense the grief of the people over President Kennedy's death. The mood of this room, hung with tribal cloths of the many African nations who contributed to it, is pensive, the lighting subdued. Visitors instinctively lower their voices.

The design of the lounge is symbolic, meant to convey the atmosphere of an African village in its slanting, textured walls and angular, floating ceiling panels. The deep red-brown of the carpet suggests the richness of the soil. Rising from it, dramatically spotlighted, is a wooden sculpture of a grief-stricken Mother Earth who represents the sorrow of all Africans. The figure, sculpted by Dr. Oku Ampofo of Ghana, is called *Asase Due* or *Mother Earth, Condolences To You.*

Eye-catching wall decorations of calabashes or dried gourds are carved with bold geometric patterns. Sometimes used as fishing floats or for holding food, versatile gourds are also inked with dye made of tree bark, then hand-stamped onto cloth to create patterns such as you see here on the traditional black and white mourning cloth hanging on the adjoining wall.

The narrow blue and white cloth in the middle of the room was "printed" by the unusual "sew dye" method: cloth is tightly stitched to resist the dye so that when the stitches are removed, a pattern is revealed.

An interesting contrast of the old and the new shows up in scenes from Nigerian villages. The "old" is the deep carving on the double doors of the lounge. These 12-foot doors were made from the wood of one 700-year-old tree. Nigerian artist Lamidi Fakeye has carved scenes of his native village, complete with a villager clutching a squawking chicken and a serving pot.

The "new" village scene, in the anteroom, is a bas-relief, hand-hammered on pearl-grey aluminum. Its work is as finely detailed as Pointillism. This small room also has a bold tapestry from Senegal, a mohair rug from Lesotho, and a bright blanket from Mali that reminds older visitors of grandma's patchwork quilt. Young visitors perk up their ears when they learn that they're in the very room that the Secret Service uses as its headquarters when the president comes to the theater.

At the black-tie unveiling of the African Lounge in 1977, attended by President and Mrs. Carter, Ghanian drummers entertained while guests dined on typical African dishes of spiced lamb fricasse and ground nut stew.

The sparkling room that contrasts with the solemn dignity of the African rooms is officially called the South Opera Lounge, but is known more fondly as

Grief manifest. Mother Earth, *mourning for a slain president and friend, is a focal point of the African Lounge.*

In the African Lounge (opposite) scenes of a Nigerian village are carved into doors made from one 700-year-old tree.

51 *Curtain Up!*

The South Opera Lounge, decorated with tapestries from Spain, is the scene of many champagne cork-popping festivities beneath the glittering Waterford crystal chandelier.

The Waterford Lounge because of the magnificent Waterford crystal chandelier that's suspended from its domed, gold-leafed ceiling.

A gift from Ireland, the brilliant chandelier, eight feet high and eight feet in diameter, weighs 1,008 pounds, and has 116 bulbs whose light is reflected in 4,000 hand-cut, hand-polished crystal prisms that have been heard to softly "sing" when stirred by gentle air currents. The chandelier and four matching wall sconces are dazzlingly reflected in a massive mirror covering most of the rear wall.

The side walls are hung with large tapestries that are a gift of Spain. They're reproductions of lively scenes of daily life by the 19th-century Spanish painter, Goya. On the right is a typical market scene, *The Crockery Vendor.* Opposite it is *The Grape Harvest,* under a bright Castilian sky. The lounge, used for receptions, cast parties and by Golden Circle members (annual contributors of $2,500 or more) was recently redecorated and relighted. This project involved much crawling around on catwalks above the lounge to study the electrical system. "It was like a scene from *Phan-*

tom of the Opera," says Victor Shargai, a founding member of the Golden Circle and the designer who coordinated the refurbishment. In the process he tore a suit "to shreds" in the tight, dusty crawl spaces, but it was all for the sake of beauty. The new lighting enhances the soft blues, greens and golds of the Spanish tapestries. The light also reveals tell-tale signs of years of festivities: the gold-leaf of the domed ceiling bears the soft scuff marks of hundreds of popped champagne corks.

A charming anteroom to the lounge is lighted by smaller Waterford chandeliers whose light glances off two five-foot-tall, brass lamps from Sri Lanka. Shaped like stylized trees whose branches end in small bowls to hold oil and wick, the lamps, purely decorative here, traditionally are lighted for auspicious occasions. Their light, symbolizing wisdom, banishes darkness.

The focal point of the room is a 17th-century still life of a silver tea service. A gift of the Netherlands, it's by P.G. Van Roestraeten, son-in-law of Franz Hals. In those days afternoon tea was popular, especially accompanied by a "grace cup," a spot of wine or whiskey—to aid digestion, so it was claimed. When the Netherlands' ambassador presented the painting at a reception in the South Opera Lounge, the "grace cup" tradition was upheld: sherry was served.

Time now to move along the Grand Foyer to the next stop, the Eisenhower Theater.

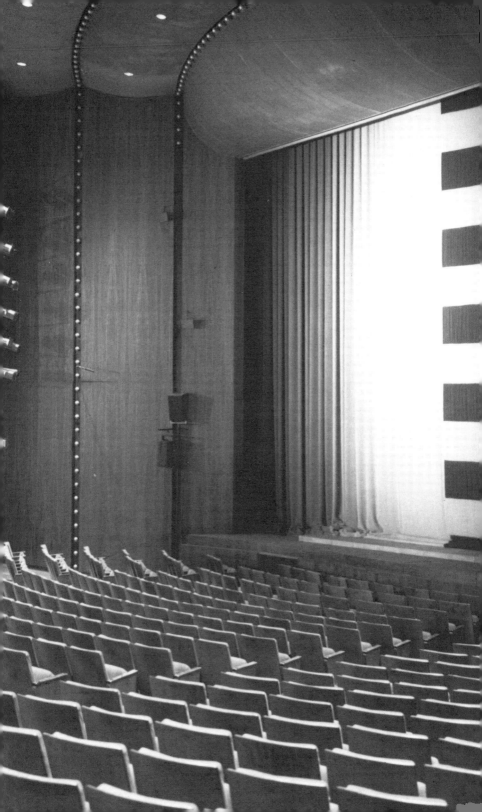

5 The Play's the Thing

Stimulate children's interest in art!

This is practically a mantra at the Kennedy Center. Kids are encouraged to look closely at their surroundings and not to be afraid to ask about what they see—even if their questions come straight out of left field like the one about the bronze bust over the entrance to the Eisenhower Theater: "Hey, who's the bald dude?"

The answer, of course, is President Eisenhower who, in 1958, signed the bill authorizing the building of a National Culture Center.

The Texas State Society, proud that "Ike" was the first Texan-born president, gave the bust to the Center. It was created by the well-known sculptor Felix de Weldon, who has captured the president's smiling face, a face much more "congenial" than "dude-y."

The bold geometric pattern of its curtain is an eye-pleasing contrast to the Eisenhower Theater's gently contoured and lined (for acoustics) ceiling.

The dedication ceremony in March 1972 was a lively occasion with a number of prominent Texans on hand including Governor John Connally and Senators Lloyd Bentsen and John Tower. Julie Nixon Eisenhower accepted the bust on behalf of the Center, and the halls resounded with the Army Band's spirited rendition of "The Eyes of Texas."

From the moment you enter the Eisenhower Theater you feel cozy and cocooned and ready for some good drama. With only 1,100 seats, the smallest of the three theaters on the main level, the Eisenhower has that sense of intimacy that nurtures actor-audience rapport. The mood is due largely to the subdued lighting—no grand chandeliers here—by the warm, nut-brown color of the East Indian laurel wood walls and the red upholstered ceiling. Imagine the richness of a red-velvet lined jewel box.

"Dramatic" is the key word for the theaters' 1,000-pound, 34-by-44-foot handwoven pure wool curtain, a gift from Canada. Half fiery-red and half stark-black, its center panels are interlaced in a bold pattern symbolic of "the unity of all nations in friendship and progress," according to its designer, Madame Mariette Rousseau Vermette. In fact, the interlocking red and black panels look very much like a column of gigantic block-letter "E's"—appropriate for the Eisenhower Theater—and that's how most patrons see it. The striking design is so popular that it's been reproduced on Kennedy Center tote bags. Just behind this dramatic stage curtain is a thick, steel fire curtain that weighs 6,000 pounds and serves as a safety curtain in the event of a backstage fire.

Since opening with Ibsen's *A Doll's House*, the Eisenhower Theater has staged more than 200 plays ranging from *A Midsummer Night's Dream*, *The Skin of Our Teeth* and *On Golden Pond* to *The Piano Lesson* and *The Search for Signs of Intelligent Life in the Universe*, plus many Washington Opera productions.

Backstage at the "Ike," as it's called by the stagehands, is the large, comfortable Green Room, softly carpeted in charcoal grey, lighted by two chandeliers and furnished with plush-covered sofas and a big, old-fashioned piano. Steeped in theatrical nostalgia, the room—painted white, not green—is "wallpapered" with row upon row of colorful posters of every show that has ever been staged at the "Ike." The room is the rest-and-relaxation center for cast and crew during their off-stage and off-duty time. "The origin of the term Green Room has been lost in the mists of time. Some long-ago, off-stage room may have been painted green, and the name stuck," says Leo Gallenstein, Supervisor of Theater Operations.

Just off-stage of the Eisenhower Theater is a "star" dressing room, the only dressing room on stage level in the entire building. It's surprisingly small and plain with a simple dressing table and lighted make-up mirror. Its big advantage is that it's practically on stage. Here it was that Elizabeth Taylor prepared for her role in *The Little Foxes*. A level below the stage are more dressing rooms for principals and chorus plus a special hairdressing room and a full laundry, minus dry cleaning facilities, for care of the costumes. (All the theaters have their own laundries, even the little Theater Lab.)

Because the Eisenhower Theater is a "road house", that is, it primarily presents shows that have been designed and built elsewhere, it has an unusually large backstage area for the relatively small size of the theater. The huge space makes the theater extremely adaptable and accommodates the hundreds of huge traveling "road boxes" filled with sound and light equipment that come with each show. The ample space also permits staging shows in repertory as the Washington Opera has done in the past. When three different productions were staged on successive nights, the scenery pieces not in use were simply stashed backstage and/or hung in the fly space directly behind the stage. They had only to be hauled out and lowered with ease when needed.

The fly space, which soars to 82 feet above the stage, is thickly criss-crossed with an intricate gridiron of black pipes, the framework on which the lights and scenery are hung. It's a tricky business. For every pound of weight in lights and scenery, there must be two pounds of counterbalance. Because the "Ike" doesn't have computers and machines for this work, it's done manually by strong, skilled stagehands perched on the flyfloor about 30 feet above the stage, an old-fashioned touch that adds a bit of drama to this special theater.

The "Ike" is nothing if not versatile. It's equipped with a projector which, in the early years of the theater, was used when elegant movie premiers were held here. Now it offers a way to enhance stage effects by projecting images onto walls or scenery. In another bit of flexibility, by removing the first three rows of theater seats, it's possible to lower a portion of the floor to create an orchestra pit so that opera, ballet and musicals can be staged here. The floor can also be raised to stage level to increase the size of the stage for larger productions. During the Center's salute to Germany in 1992, this adaptable theater metamorphosed into a 1930s Berlin Cabaret with part of the audience sitting at candlelit tables on the stage, just inches from high kicking chorus girls. (Not all performances take place on stage: a teen-age chorus from North Carolina on a tour of the Center stood in the aisle of the Eisenhower Theater and harmonized *America The Beautiful* for an audience of two, an usher and a tour guide. "There, we've sung at the Kennedy Center," their director said proudly.)

Another smiling President Eisenhower greets you on the box tier level, this time in an Anthony Wills painting over the entrance to the president's box. The "twin" of this painting hangs in the White House, for Ike liked the work so much that he asked Mr. Wills to paint his official portrait for the White House's gallery of presidents.

Don't be surprised to see youngsters walking back and forth in front of the painting. They're just testing the president's glance which "follows" them from side to side.

Two ancient works of art grace the box tier level. Both are containers, but they couldn't be more different in their backgrounds—one from the working classes, the other from royalty.

The first, on the north end, is Cyprus' gift to the Center, an amphora or ancient shipping container that dates back to about 800 B.C. Those were days of glory for the bold sailors of Cyprus who ventured to every port of the known world, the holds of their ships bulging with racks of amphora, all brimful of olive oil, grain, fruits and wine. Of those hundreds of thousands of simple pottery containers, the one that has reached the Kennedy Center was decorated by an artist centuries ago, its original white color overpainted in light brown with a darker brown abstract design. Why? A special occasion? Who did it? What goods have been shipped in the amphora? What exotic ports has it visited? Only 15 inches high, the ancient amphora holds more mystery than can be imagined.

The container with the royal pedigree, displayed on a pedestal in front of the president's box, is a lustrous alabaster vase once owned by King Djeser of Egypt's Third Dynasty who ruled from the ancient capital of Memphis around 2680 B.C.

In October 1975, Mrs. Anwar Sadat presented the vase to the Center on behalf of the people of Egypt. It's a particularly fitting gift for a national culture center because the king, its original owner, probably would have felt right at home in Washington and the Kennedy Center. Not only was he skilled in politics—he developed an administrative system for a fully unified Egypt—but he was also a patron of the arts and a leader in the flowering of Egyptian culture. Moreover, as founder of the Sakkara stepped pyramid, he undoubtedly knew about the problems and pressures of constructing a great memorial. Today, his fragile vase, in amazingly good condition, is a lovely 4,500 year-old link between the ancient and modern cultures.

Two vibrant tapestries adorn the stairwells of the Eisenhower Theater. Titled, *Poem to Fire One* and *Poem to Fire Two*, they're based on paintings of one of Mexico's leading artists, Leonardo Nierman, whose works typically blaze with color. In one tapestry, red-orange flames spew from dark depths with volcanic force. The second tapestry, whose flames lick wildly across the "canvas," reminds many music lovers of Wagner's *Ring* opera—Brunnhilde on her fire-encircled rock. Not everyone sees flames, however. One solemn little girl protested softly to her tour guide, "I don't see any flames," she whispered. "I see horses racing over the fields." Another child saw swans with their wings outspread.

The official name of the lounge adjacent to the Eisenhower Theater is the George Rogers Clark room. A bronze statue of the early American soldier by Felix de Weldon stands at the entryway. But most people know the room as "the bird room" because of its treasury of porcelain birds from the world-renowned Boehm studios in Trenton, New Jersey.

Actually much more than birds peep out of the handsome breakfronts that line the walls of the lounge. There's a whole world of wildlife in porcelain—bees, foxes, bobcat cubs, flowers, fish, butterflies, grasshoppers and even frogs, snails, beetles and ladybugs—all reproduced in extraordinary, true-to-nature detail right down to the laciest fin of an angelfish and the thin veins in an iris petal.

The collection is a gift of two couples, Mr. and Mrs. Oliver Delchamps, Sr., of Alabama and Dr. and Mrs. Samuel Lombardo of Florida. The custom-made dis-

The highlight of the George Rogers Clark Lounge—a mute swan, one of a pair from the Boehm porcelain studios, is perfectly detailed down to the smallest wisp of a feather.

play cabinets were given by Mrs. Helen F. Boehm, the widow of the artist, Edward M. Boehm.

All the animals in the cases speak for the extraordinary "TLC" (tender, loving care) given them by a man whose passion was to recreate the beauty of nature with absolute fidelity in porcelain. On his farm Edward Boehm surrounded himself with dozens of domestic and wild animals and even had a huge, climate-controlled aviary of exotic birds. His weekly food shopping list included hundreds of pounds of seeds, berries, fruits, fish and vegetables, plus vitamins and minerals, plus 30,000 worms! Fortunately, his beloved animals earned their keep as artist's models.

As you enter the room, you're immediately drawn to a large, lighted glass case in which a magnificent pure white male swan hovers protectively with outstretched wings over his resting mate and three fluff-ball cygnets. The swans are mute swans, birds whose beauty and tranquility have made them a symbol of peace. There's a lovely story behind this family scene.

This sculpture is a small version of the original Mute Swans which the artists in the Boehm studio created as a commemorative piece after the death of Edward Boehm at age 55 in 1969. The original sculpture was life size. The wing span of the male swan was seven and a half feet. To produce a porcelain sculpture so monumental and challenging and to uphold Edward Boehm's standards of perfection took two years of work by a team of 11 artists. They cast the swans in 509 mold sections using eight tons of plaster, then carved 60,000 individual feather barbs on the swans' wings.

The majestic sculpture was unveiled in Washington, D.C. in March 1971, after which it was exhibited in American embassies in London, Brussels, Bonn and Paris. In February 1972, on President Nixon's *Journey of Peace* to China, he presented the swans to Chairman Mao as the official gift of the United States to the people of China.

A limited edition of 5,000 *Bird of Peace* plates was issued to celebrate the swan sculpture. One of them is on display in the lounge in the case to the left of the swan family. It's a 13-inch plate of bone porcelain painted in fifteen delicate colors, with an incised border filled with pure gold.

Tucked alongside the cases of porcelain is a little clear plastic donation box. Insignificant amid the surrounding beauty, it nevertheless fills with a fair amount of "thank you" money from visitors, gifts that help support the Center's extensive educational and half-price ticket programs, which are described in later chapters.

Now it's time to move along to the two small theaters on the roof terrace level and learn about the mysterious caterwauling that once rang through the rafters up there.

6 Fiddlers—and Actors— On the Roof

Maybe you've heard of Mosby, the clever, wild, grey cat who lived in the Kennedy Center for about five years. He was famous in his time. He was written up in newspapers, and his life's story is told in a charming young person's book, *Mosby, The Kennedy Center Cat*, by Beppie Noyes.

Mosby apparently was one of dozens of wild cats that lived on the construction site. Somehow he must have been trapped in the building when the foundation was laid. And so, he made his home in the Terrace Theater. At that time it was nothing more than a huge, dusty attic because the Center, having run out of money, had put construction of that part of the building on "hold."

With its exposed beams and dozens of niches to hide in, the empty shell made an ideal spot for a cat except that there was no constant source of food and water. The situation forced Mosby to become a tiny swift-moving shadow and sneak-thief *par excellence* who, in the blink of an eye, could snatch lobster, shrimp, caviar, paté—even chicken halves—from the elegant buffet tables that the restaurant staff set up for fund-raising luncheons and cocktail parties. These gourmet meals were sporadic, however, reducing Mosby's dining to a dwindling supply of mice.

Fortunately, Mosby's presence and hide-out were discovered. Cat lovers on the Center's staff gave him his name and provided him with daily food and drink, which he magnanimously accepted though he rarely deigned to show himself and even more rarely allowed his fur to be stroked.

Mosby discovered that by nestling on a tiny platform in the false ceiling above the Eisenhower Theater which is directly below the Terrace Theater, he had a bird's eye view of the stage. He became a fan of drama, ballet and opera. Unfortunately, he expressed his love of the arts by howling—great drawn out yowls that echoed eerily through the air conditioning vents. Although some actors thought that Mosby brought good luck, orders came down from the powers-that-be to catch and evict the noisy cat. The Center, after all, had a prestigious position to uphold. The eviction notice led to some lively adventures, all of which are delightfully chronicled in Mrs. Noyes' book. To this day long-time Kennedy Center employees speak fondly of old Mosby.

Though most people don't know it, the Center is not without a cat. Down near the loading docks, tucked into a closet in the gift shop offices, is the home of Sam, complete with food dishes, kitty litter box, scratching post and toys. Like Mosby, Sam is basically a loner. Unlike Mosby he's totally disinterested in the arts. Someone, sometime, brought Sam in as a mouser, and now that his task is done, his only interest is in the good, pampered life of lots of food and cat naps in out-of-the-way corners behind stacks of supplies. Sam, who is yellow-eyed, sleek and black, is a genuine Kennedy Center Fat Cat.

The lack of funds that halted construction and made it possible for Mosby to enjoy his cavernous "attic" came to an end in 1976 when the people of Japan gave the United States a Bicentennial birthday gift. Three million dollars to build a theater in the empty concrete shell! It took its name—Terrace Theater—from its location on the top floor or roof terrace level. (Creative youngsters have asked why it's not called The Mosby Theater.)

After two and a half years of work, the theater, at one end of the North Gallery, was dedicated on Sunday, January 28, 1979. Prime Minister of Japan, Mayayoshi Ohira, sent a message of hope that the theater would symbolize the "universality of the performing arts and of Japanese-American friendship."

The opening night audience included First Lady Rosalynn Carter and daughter Amy, Kennedy Center Board Chairman, Roger L. Stevens, Martin Feinstein, Executive Director of Performing Arts, and His Excellency Fumihiko Togo, Ambassador of Japan.

They were treated to a special occasion, an opening night unlike any other in the city. For the Terrace Theater wasn't just dedicated, it was purified in an ancient Shinto ritual. To perform it, the Japanese government sent a 36-man Grand Kabuki Troupe from Tokyo, including two "Living National Treasures," actor/dancer Nakamura Kanzanburo and musician Hinatayu Takemoto.

The ceremonies began with a ritual called "Kokera-Otoshi" meaning "opening" in which ceremonially costumed Kabuki actors, accompanied by flutes and hand drums, performed solemn dances and chanted prayers for the prosperity of the new theater. In traditional, stylized gestures, they scattered salt on the stage as a rite of purification—and possibly also for good luck in attracting big audiences in the same way that many Japanese restaurant owners put salt outside their door to attract customers.

The solemn ceremony then turned lively with a Double Lion Dance. A father lion in flowing white silk mane and a child lion with a huge red mane told a Japanese legend in dynamic dancing and cavorting. Small Double Lion dolls are showcased in the lobby of the Terrace, as well as a priceless antique silk wedding kimono embroidered with chrysanthemums, symbols of the Japanese Imperial family.

The opening of the Terrace Theater meant much more than adding another 500 seats to the Center. As Roger Stevens remarked that night, the new, small theater allowed the Center to "fully meet our Congressional mandate . . . to provide . . . a broad range of programming . . . and expand efforts in education and public service." Here was a perfect, affordable theater for presentations of small dance companies, string quartets, chamber opera, jazz ensembles, poetry readings, lecture series, musical soloists, innovative drama and productions of unknown works by new talents that would bring in new audiences. The large stages of the main theaters were not only too expensive for small events but the acoustics weren't designed for them either.

The Terrace immediately charms people with its soft look—seats of pearl-grey plush as downy as pussywillows, plum color carpeting and softly lighted walls of silver and lilac. And the wonderful, steeply sloped seats! In this theater, you don't care if the woman in front of you wears a hat. The sight lines from every seat are that good.

But don't be deceived by the apparent simplicity of this lovely little theater. It's a unique hall, a marvel of flexibility and as acoustically excellent as the three main theaters thanks to architect Philip Johnson and, once again, Dr. Cyril Harris. What makes it unique is that it combines the features necessary for a performance stage, such as trap doors in the floor and fly spaces in which to hang scenery and lights, with the special acoustical needs of a recital hall.

The solution is ingenious: when small musical groups are on the program, false acoustical walls are rolled onto the stage, secured there and covered with a false ceiling, complete with inset lights, which is lowered from its storage space high overhead. They form an open-sided room or shell which projects the musical sounds outward and keeps them from soaring up and getting trapped in the fly space.

The hallmark of the Terrace is its intimacy. That comes not alone from its small size, but also from its steeply sloped auditorium that brings the seats close to the stage. Performers praise it as much as the audience does. Each feels that he or she is alone with the other. The responsiveness between them is almost palpable.

The Terrace is home to many popular musical series including the Washington Chamber Orchestra, the string, piano and jazz series of the Washington Performing Arts Society, Terrace Concerts, Theater Chamber Players, Young Concert Artists, the Washington Ballet, Dance America, American College Festival, and varied shows for youngsters from pre-school through high school.

Backstage, the Terrace has several bright, modern dressing rooms and an acoustically-designed rehearsal room that's so well soundproofed that small groups can rehearse even when performers are on stage. Dancers also warm up here at the barre. The hallways, like those throughout the Center, are decorated with posters of past productions, but in this theater's "Green

Room," the walls are papered with oriental designs of delicate, plum blossoms.

As you leave the Terrace Theater on your way to the Theater Lab directly across the hall, notice the two unusual planters containing *ficus* trees. A gift of Portugal, the planters are made of that country's famous, intricately decorated tile. The patterns of the large, deeply sculpted pieces, designed by Mario de Silva, have a Moorish richness, highlighted with bold shades of blue.

Among the Center's six theaters, the 400-seat Theater Lab is unique. In theatrical terms it's a "black box stage," a simple, large space with black floor, black ceiling and "walled" with black curtains. As flexible and adaptive as a woman's "basic black" outfit that can be dressed up or down, the theater can take on many configurations by the simple task of moving sections of bench-like seats, rearranging lights and shifting stage platforms, depending on production needs.

The Theater Lab is one of the most used spaces in the Center. With an average of 18 productions a week, day and night, the Lab has a lot of foot traffic. Most of it is little feet. Thousands of excited youngsters come by the school bus load for free performances especially programmed for young people. The performances are a skillful weave of entertainment and education—fairy tales and musicals based on themes of ecology, history and classical literature performed by large, singing-and-dancing puppets; plays acted in music and mime; plays in sign language; plays about courageous men and women; and even plays written by young students for their peers as part of the Young Playwrights Festival.

The Theater Lab's name derives from the late 1970s when it was an experimental theater space housing The Musical Theater Lab, a joint project of the Stuart Ostrow Foundation and the Kennedy Center whose primary purpose was to mount workshop productions of musicals-in-development. The workshops were a kind of out-of-town rehearsal period with actors in rehearsal clothes working on a stage with simple lighting and minimal scenery. The project was a unique, experimental one with emphasis on improving material-in-the-works in order to encourage growth and innovation in American musical theater. The multi-purpose, "black box" space on the Center's roof level was ideal for the Lab.

For a year and a half in the early 1980s, the Theater Lab was home to the American National Theater project under the direction of Peter Sellars who produced sometimes controversial but always provocative and exciting programs. Currently, for eight performances a week, the Theater Lab rocks with the laughter of audiences at *Shear Madness*, a comedy whodunit that has been packing people into the theater for nearly seven years. The adaptability of the Theater Lab allows the single-room set of the adult mystery to be rolled in and out of position to make way for the young peoples' daytime performances.

At the far end of the Gallery from the Terrace Theater and Theater Lab is a cheerful, pleasant room with the most deep-down comfortable seats in the building. It's the Performing Arts Library (PAL), a joint project of the Library of Congress and the Kennedy Center. The primary mission of the PAL, which is staffed by library specialists in the performing arts, is to serve as a research and information source for the staff and patrons of the Center as well as for creative artists involved in productions here. Its extensive collection contains some 5,000 reference books, 450 periodicals and more than 6,000 recordings and videotapes. As a section of the Music Division of the Library of Congress, the PAL has a computer terminal and audio link to its parent library as well as to other electronic library networks, so researchers can quickly identify and locate creative and resource materials. As tour guides tell visitors, "If you're looking for something that has anything at all to do with performing arts, this is the place to find it." Besides its research mission, the bright and inviting library serves another role. Over the years, it has become a kind of small, neighborhood library for people in near-by apartments, including the Watergate. Many are "regulars" who pop in every day to chat with librarians, to relax in the deep seats and browse through the daily newspapers.

Between the North and South Galleries on the top

floor (which correspond to the Halls of Nations and States on the main level) is a huge, high-ceilinged room called the Atrium. Thanks to skylights designed for noise control, the Atrium has a light, open feeling. This is a popular and user-friendly room where you'll find everything from mobs of children on field trips sprawled on the floor eating brown bag lunches to elegant banquets for celebrities and visiting royalty. The King of Saudi Arabia was entertained here. There are also pre-performance lectures by composers, maestros and performing artists, plus staff meetings, training sessions, appreciation dinners for volunteers, wine and cheese parties, receptions, cast parties . . . and the list goes on. With all the food that's consumed in the Atrium, the choice of the wall-to-wall carpeting was immensely practical. No royal red carpet here; instead, the tightly-woven pattern is a mix of hues that can match almost any spill from wine to gravy to grape jelly.

The Center's two restaurants are on the tenth story roof terrace level. Before heading for a snack or dinner, pause in the South Gallery to replenish your artistic soul with a look at Australia's gift to honor President Kennedy, a set of seven brilliantly colored Aubusson tapestries woven from Australian wool. The work of John Coburn (who also did the curtains for the Sydney Opera House), the tapestries, collectively called *Seven Days*, symbolize God's creation of the world in strong, bold designs and glowing golds, hot pinks, greens and blues.

Six large Moroccan wool carpets decorate the North and South Galleries. Woven in a striking black and white geometric design, the carpets are a personal gift to the Center from King Hassan II of Morocco.

One of the best times and places in Washington to refresh tour-weary bodies is mid-afternoon in the Encore Cafe, the Kennedy Center's rooftop cafeteria. Through the windows, diners can see Washington's shining marble monuments, traffic passing over Potomac River bridges and aircraft climbing up from National Airport. Virginia's green hills lie on the horizon.

Between lunch and dinner rush hours, the 300-seat Cafe is quiet except for the murmurs of a few scattered diners, some of them willowy dancers or musicians poring over orchestral scores on rehearsal breaks.

At the other end of the South Gallery, the Roof Terrace restaurant, lighted by crystal chandeliers and decorated in pale greens, greys, mauves and creams, also has superb views. Its menus reflect the Center's role as the nation's performing arts center by featuring foods from different regions of the country such as Florida Key Lime Pie, Chesapeake Bay Crab Cakes and Southwestern Chicken Quesadilla (tortilla-type pancakes with cheese and spicy chicken). Occasional "Theme Menus" may be offered during special presentations such as Viennese Sachertorte (extra rich chocolate cake) during the National Symphony Orchestra's *Mozart Summer Music Festival.* Adjoining the restaurant is an intimate lounge, the Hors D'Oeuvrerie, where theater-goers head for drinks, light meals and sweets.

Like proverbial postmen who aren't stopped by sleet or snow, camera-toting visitors brave wind and rain, if necessary, to snap pictures of Washington's best scenery from the roof terrace. While you're strolling the roof terrace, look for Tunisia's gift to the Center, a mosaic atop a small raised platform just outside the door of the South Gallery near the entrance to the Encore Cafe. Formed by thousands of pastel-colored stones, the poet Virgil, flanked by two muses, is shown holding a papyrus roll on which is written his epic poem, the *Aeneid.* The mosaic is a reproduction of the original which dates from the second century, long after the poet's death, and is treasured as the only likeness of him in existence.

The ledge that keeps exuberant sightseers from toppling off the roof is capped by a hedge of Japanese holly bushes, some of the 3,600 shrubs that beautify the Center's landscape. These tough little shrubs are remarkable. In true theater trouper fashion, they perform under all conditions. Throughout Washington's icy winters, baking summers and year-round drying winds, the hollies keep going strong.

Now it's time to head downstairs and stroll outside for a longer look at the landscape and four unusual outdoor sculptures that adorn it.

7 The Arts Alfresco

"People eat and drink on the River Terrace? At a memorial to a president?" an amazed visitor once exclaimed.

It's true—delightfully so. The memorial's park-like setting invites strolling and picnicking. With its food carts and gourmet picnic boxes, the Center actually encourages patrons to dine alfresco on the River Terrace next to the fountains and under the weeping willows, in a picturesque scene *a la* Monet.

Besides the 3,600 shrubs, about 350 trees dot the 17 acres of land that surround the Center. All of it is tended by National Park Service landscape gardeners with assistance from half a dozen dedicated volunteers who weed, trim ivy, pick up trash and generally help to keep the place tidy.

A view from the Potomac on a warm summer day—the River Terrace, gracefully lined with weeping willows.

From day one, the Kennedy Center plans called for a park-like setting. Maintaining that setting with year-round color remains an important goal. With the changing seasons, the building is encircled in turn by blossoming tulips, daffodils, Bradford Pear and flowering cherry trees, magnolias, marigolds, wax begonias and winter-blooming Chinese Plum trees. Trees of multi-hued greens that shade the sloping lawns and river banks include pin oaks, maples, dogwoods, crab apples, willow oaks, and, of course, the 64 dramatic weeping willows on the River Terrace. Vibrant green holly trees in large planters on the wide plazas provide contrasting color and texture to the Center's gleaming marble facade.

As green uniforms are the trademark of the Park Service workers, bright yellow caps are the trademark of volunteer gardeners. But they're more than head protection; they are the volunteer's identification and passport to the flower beds. Before the caps were de rigueur, one weed-pulling volunteer was berated for being a flower thief by a civic-minded passer-by. Indoors, when the volunteers shake the ornamental *ficus* trees in the Grand Foyer, their yellow caps identify them as legitimate gardeners who are knocking off dead leaves, not a bunch of angry people taking out their aggressions on helpless plants.

The gardeners, staff and volunteers alike, meet all kinds of people, including early-morning joggers who come to put in their mileage (four times around the Center is about a mile) as well as one gentleman who was found digging in the raised flower beds for what he claimed are the biggest and best fishing worms in Washington. Volunteer gardener Betsy Randolph recalls another passing gentleman who cautioned her against working too hard. "I think of the Center as my house. I like to keep it tidy," she replied. "I can relate to that," he said with a smile—and she realized he was Mr. Kennedy Center himself, Roger L. Stevens!

Set amid the trees and flower beds are several monumental sculptures that are also gifts from other countries. From Germany, facing the front Plaza entrances, are two massive bronze reliefs titled *America* and *War Or Peace* whose themes raised a few eyebrows when the bronzes were presented in 1971. The work of German sculptor Jurgen Weber, they're intended to question where man's intelligence will lead him when it's pressured by technical and economic forces—to the destruction of the world or to more creative power?

In 1991, the people of Uruguay presented the Kennedy Center with a tall, bright sculpture which, by a bit of serendipity, exactly matches the riotous yellow-orange of marigold beds which surround it on the Center's north lawn, across from the Watergate.

How to describe this sculpture by Alfredo Halegua who has enigmatically titled it *Pie in the Sky?* A "gigantic cubistic banana," one theater-goer commented. Imagine large metal blocks in the shapes of triangles, rectangles and rhomboids stacked upon one another to form an angular tower which, despite its size and bulk, is actually whimsical. When given a firm push, the big yellow tower s-l-o-w-l-y rotates on its narrow base causing all angles and patches of light and shadow on its surfaces to shift and create wholly new patterns.

If you approach the Center from across the front lawn (which at this writing is a temporary parking lot while the underground garage is being renovated), you'll walk under the hooves of a high-rearing horse. He and his rider, carrying a 12-foot steel lance, burst heroically from a massive block of stone. It's Don Quixote astride Rosinante, the stable horse who served as the Don's noble steed. The unusual sculpture in which Rosinante and the fictional knight-errant are at the crest of a flying charge is the gift of Spain and the work of Aurelio Teno. Twenty feet tall and weighing 66 tons in bronze, stone and pink marble, the dramatic sculpture was presented to the Kennedy Center by King Juan Carlos and Queen Sofia. Passers-by often speculate about Rosinante's jagged, broken hoof. The work of vandals? No. The break is intentional. It symbolizes the frustrated hopes of Cervantes' romantic, unrealistic hero.

Don Quixote astride his "charger" provides a dramatic approach to the Center.

The south circular drive of the Center, a tree-bordered expanse of lawn that slopes toward the river, is dominated by the gift from Colombia, an untitled, black aluminum sculpture by Eduardo Ramirez. Despite its monumental size (4,000 pounds, 11 feet high, 11 feet wide and 20 feet long), the open-work piece conveys a sense of lightness and forward motion. Both day and night, under sunlight and spotlight, the sculpture offers changing patterns of light, shadow and movement. Its sleek, black angles contrast pleasingly with the clean-lined white building beside it.

Now let's head back inside that building for a glimpse into the busy, overstuffed, honeycomb of office and storage space behind the Center's serene marble walls.

8 Behind the Scenes

When eager new volunteers finish their training, they're often advised to wander behind the scenes, through the innards of the Kennedy Center, to see it, hear it, smell it and experience its energy firsthand. On occasion they've been laughingly warned that unless they leave a trail of bread crumbs, they may wander for hours in the maze of corridors, alcoves, rehearsal rooms, storage compartments, cubby holes, vast backstage areas, cramped understage areas, narrow passageways, nooks, niches, crannies and countless doors, elevators and stairways.

Just what are these wandering volunteers likely to see and hear when they stealthily open doors just a crack and peek inside? Very likely, they'll see actors blocking a play in a bare rehearsal room. Tense young dancers in tights may be sweating through a tough audition or ballerinas in leg warmers stretching at the barre. Elsewhere lone musicians or full orchestras bend over their instruments for hours on end. Singers trill up and down the octaves. Stagehands haul and hang scenery. Sound and light technicians push buttons and levers amid noises and blinking lights at modules of high-tech equipment. The Board of Trustees may huddle in serious discussions in lounge rooms. Wardrobe custodians wash, iron and repair costumes and comb out wigs. Ushers slip into red jackets getting ready to go on duty. Volunteers chat at long tables while they stuff envelopes. Upstairs, in scores of cubicle offices, the work of programming, scheduling, advertising, ticketing and education goes on apace. And everyone, at one time or another, stops by the canteen for a coffee break or hot meal.

Housekeeping and maintenance is never-ending. Between 6,000 and 12,000 people tromp over the Center's carpets every day, tracking in whatever's in season—dirt, mud, snow and water. They smudge the walls, railings, marble and mirrors with millions of fingerprints, and discard bins full of paper and plastic trash after every performance. Spiders, too, love the Center and weave webs wherever there's an inviting nook or cranny. The bust of President Kennedy offers many of those. The bust must be dusted weekly or become misty-grey with spider webbing.

According to Park Ranger Susan Creger, who monitors the housekeeping contract, the theaters are cleaned after every show. All 19,000 square yards of carpet are vacuumed daily (some parts twice a day). They are cleaned and stretched tighter as the need arises, and are replaced about every four years. Wear and tear comes not just from the pitter-patter of some 20,000 big and little feet every day. Rolling equipment like strollers, wheelchairs, vendors' carts, rolling scaffolds, heavy-duty luggage racks take their toll. There is even a sewing machine on wheels that's rolled out when the heavy, metal-threaded drapes begin to sag and need re-hemming.

One of the biggest jobs, tackled only once a year, is cleaning the chandeliers and mirrors in the Grand Foyer. Each of the twelve prisms in each of the 64 units of each of the 18 chandeliers, plus the prisms in the 22 wall sconces, is taken out and dipped. That's almost 16,000 prisms. Workers polish the 58-foot high Belgian mirrors while standing atop a telescopic scaffold. The lower parts of the mirrors are cleaned frequently of fingerprints and even occasional noseprints of toddlers who delight in pressing their faces against such a big wonderful looking glass. Periodically, to banish thousands more fingerprints, the Center's yards and yards of bronze handrails are buffed until they gleam like thick ropes of buttery-gold pulled taffy.

Keeping marble floors as glossy as wet ice is another huge, on-going job. Cracked, chipped or buckled marble might be repaired by the staff stone mason. If sections need replacement, new marble to match the original is ordered from Italy.

While things are kept clean and repaired by the housekeeping and maintenance departments, they're safe-guarded and monitored with cameras and alarms by the country's oldest uniformed law enforcement agency, the U.S. Park Police. The officers who patrol the Center's halls and grounds trace their roots back to 1791 when George Washington created the young country's first uniformed law enforcers, then called Park Watchmen. Judging from the number of questions about the president's safety when he comes to see a show, one can tell that the assassination of President Lincoln at Ford's Theatre has made a deep impression on school kids.

"When the president comes to the theater, it's a whole new ballgame where security is concerned," says Lt. Philip Kramer, Commander of the U.S. Park Police at the Kennedy Center. From five or six officers on duty, the number jumps to 120 plus about 25 plainclothes Secret Service personnel. Every door and every entry is closely watched. Two hours before the president arrives (not through the public entrances), the corridors and theater, including backstage, are cleared out. Police dogs come in and make a thorough sweep of the area. Next comes the installation of metal detectors—as many as eight plus numerous hand held ones—in the corridors and backstage. Only then, after everything is "sanitized," are staff, stagehands, actors and audience allowed inside.

The Park Police stationed at the Center when the building opened in 1971 faced a unique problem: visitors liked the building so much that they came, they saw and they snatched souvenirs. They lifted marble handles from faucets in the restroom, swatches from the golden drapes in the Grand Foyer, chunks from the red carpeting, even crystal chandelier prisms. This was souvenir collecting on a grand scale. "Collectors" even brought their own knives and scissors to attack the carpets and drapes.

"It was vandalism, but not malicious vandalism. It was the Kennedy mystique," says longtime Opera House Manager Richard Kidwell, expressing the popular view of the phenomenon. "The aura of the Kennedy era still lingered. People needed some part of the slain president, and in their enthusiasm they nearly stripped the chandeliers in the elevators bare." (The elevators are now lighted more practically by cut-glass globe fixtures.) The destruction was so bad that the Center was closed to tourists for three months until security could be tightened.

Today, vandalism isn't a problem thanks to enhanced security, the passage of time, the opening of souvenir shops and, not least of all, the presence of the ushers, a band of red-coated men and women who are sprinkled as generously throughout the Center as cherries in a Christmas cake. Stationed behind velvet ropes at the theater entrances for most of the day and evening, they guard against theft and rowdiness. As traffic directors, they help with the smooth shepherding of tour groups, round up stragglers and generally keep a sharp eye. Most are knowledgeable about the art works they guard and protect their turf with the zeal of a lioness with cubs—upholding their reputation as security's first line of defense.

ARTS

9 The Triple A's: Artistic Affiliates and Associates

If you should open an unmarked door on one of the Center's lower levels, you may be startled by what appears to be a double row of Egyptian mummy cases. A closer look reveals that the cases, far from being associated with the dead, are actually symbols of vigorous life. They are the packing cases for the cellos and bass viols of the National Symphony Orchestra and, like the decal-plastered luggage of seasoned travelers, they're covered with the multi-colored labels and logos of foreign countries and international airlines—testimony that the National Symphony Orchestra is alive and well, sharing its music with people around the world.

Founded in 1931 by Hans Kindler, who was also its first music director, the NSO is Washington's oldest performing arts institution. Its early years were full of struggle in a city where performing arts were far from the spotlight. Nonetheless, the orchestra not only performed concert series in Constitution Hall but, with the strong support of its Women's Committee, developed and expanded an educational program for young people, including the Tiny Tots children's concerts.

When the Kennedy Center opened in 1971, the NSO became its resident orchestra. Antal Dorati became its third music director after Hans Kindler and Howard Mitchell. With the superb, acoustically excellent Concert Hall as its home, the NSO would gain international prominence and acclaim. World-renowned conductor and cellist Mstislav Rostropovich became the fourth music director of the NSO in 1977. In 1986 the orchestra became affiliated with the Kennedy Center. The Center now provides financial support and some administrative services such as public relations and marketing. The NSO, with its own Board of Directors and music administration staff, is responsible for the orchestra's artistic quality as well as its private fund raising.

In addition to its ever-expanding educational programs for young people and its 52-week season of more than 200 concerts, the 103-musician orchestra performs at special events such as presidential inaugurations, visits of heads of state and Fourth of July celebrations on the west lawn of the Capitol. Besides all this, it regularly packs its bags, including those well-traveled "mummy cases" and takes its beautiful sounds on tour around the world. The itinerary includes four tours of Europe, three of the Far East, two to South America and five tours around the United States. One of the most memorable was the famous, emotional and triumphant 1990 journey to the U.S.S.R., the homeland from which Maestro Rostropovich had been exiled in 1974 because of his work for humanitarian causes. The orchestra made a second, highly acclaimed tour to Russia in the fall of 1993 at the start of the Maestro's final season after 16 years as music director.

In the recording field, the orchestra won its first international recording prize under Maestro Dorati. In fact, under his baton, the orchestra's first nine recordings won six major awards. Under the leadership of Maestro Rostropovitch, who was named *Musical America*'s 1987 Musician of the Year for his accomplishments with the National Symphony, the orchestra's highly acclaimed recordings include the complete *Boris Godunov*, nominated for a Grammy for Best Opera Recording of 1990.

The Washington Opera also resides in the Kennedy Center in a busy warren of offices brightly decorated with opera posters. Both the Opera and American Film Institute (whose administrative offices are in the Watergate building) are independent organizations with their own staffs and boards handling their programming and funding. Their productions, along with numerous programs of the Washington Performing Arts Society, add color and spice to the Center's offerings and help to fulfill its mandate to offer a wide spectrum of classical and contemporary performing arts.

The Washington Opera traces its roots to 1956 when a few hard-working opera lovers got together, created the Opera Society of Washington and then very bravely put on a somewhat offbeat opera—Mozart's *The Abduction from the Seraglio*—in the Lisner Auditorium of The George Washington University. Despite the cramped space and shallow (for opera) stage, the production was a success.

Since that first pioneering performance, by dint of imaginative programming and a frontier spirit in producing bold new works, the Washington Opera has had increasingly successful seasons and critical commentary that sparkles with comments such as "crowning triumph," "a winner!" "compelling" and "breakthrough performance!"

In 1971, after years of scraping up financial support opera by opera, the loosely organized "company" moved into the Opera House with the world premiere of Ginastera's *Beatrix Cenci*. Within three or four years the company had a legitimate season of three operas at the Center. In 1977, the Society became The Washington Opera and moved into rented office space at the Kennedy Center.

Over the next few years, several general managers directed the company, keeping it on its path to success. Then, in 1980, the man who seemed to have been born for the job took over and the company really took off. That man is Martin Feinstein who, after 25 years with impresario Sol Hurok, served eight years as the Kennedy Center's first and only Executive Director of Performing Arts. He electrified the Opera House stage by importing exciting performances by the Bolshoi Opera, Paris Opera, Berlin Opera, La Scala and the Vienna State Opera plus the greatest ballet companies in the world. He also played a large role in getting the support of over $6 million from foreign governments for the presentation of music, dance and theater companies from abroad.

The Washington Opera's growth has been phenomenal. In 1980, on a $2 million dollar budget, the company staged 16 performances of four operas using rented sets. Twelve years later, with a budget of over $11 million, it put on 65 performances of seven operas.

In the same time it had grown from not owning a single set to designing, building and owning 34 productions. The company now has a world-class reputation that ranks with the operas of Milan, Moscow, Vienna, London and Paris.

The Washington Performing Arts Society (WPAS), founded in 1964 by impresario Patrick Hayes, is one of the leading non-profit concert presenters in the country. It leases the Center's theaters frequently enough to appear to be an affiliate, but it actually is an independent organization and leases many other theaters in the area as well. Its wide range of programming adds color and variety to the Center's—and to Washington's—stages. There's a little of everything from symphonic music and Japanese drummers to African gospel choirs and 15th-century Turkish music.

Now let's take a look at how the Center, through entertainment and education, is pursuing one of its main goals: building audiences for the future.

10 A Classroom for the Nation

On many school-day mornings, a long line of yellow school busses, like a chain of big, bright caterpillars, crawls up the hill to the Kennedy Center and releases literally thousands of Washington-area school kids.

Inside the building, the eager, curious youngsters (shepherded by chaperons into surprisingly orderly ranks) go their separate ways. Most file into the Concert Hall for a free Young People's Concert by the National Symphony Orchestra. Others sink into the plush seats of the Eisenhower Theater to learn how a drama is staged. The rest scatter through the building, some on tours of the halls and lounges, some in the Terrace Theater for a young person's look at modern dance. The littlest ones may settle in the Theater Lab for an enchanted hour of African folk tales. It's a rare day during the school year when the busses don't bring at least a few hundred children. Often as many as 5,000 swarm through the building and on really special days, 7,000.

Although the Kennedy Center is internationally recognized as one of the finest performing arts centers in the world, most people aren't aware that it's also a classroom for the country. Presenting the performing arts is only half of the Center's mission. Education is the other half. Right from the beginning it has strongly and actively supported interweaving the arts with the education of America's youth. More recently, under the leadership of Chairman James Wolfensohn and President Lawrence Wilker, even greater emphasis has been put on extending the Center's educational arm into communities and school districts across the nation.

"No education is complete without the performing arts," declares Mr. Wolfensohn. "Through performances we celebrate and reaffirm our freedom to create, to dream, to risk and to excel. We pass on our

cultural heritage to the next generation."

To do this, working in partnership with educators at all levels, the Center has developed more than a dozen pioneering education programs that reach across the country as well as deep into the local community. Their subject matter ranges far and wide through the arts. Children learn to express emotion and ideas with simple hand puppets. They take part in drama and literature workshops. There are hands-on demonstrations of musical instruments. Highly-charged competitions among talented young writers, composers, actors, designers and musicians culminate in public performances at the Center.

Imagine being young and living in an area where you have a choice of 400 performances of dance, music, opera, puppetry, storytelling and theater—all of it designed especially for young people. Youngsters who live in or near the nation's capital have that choice, and every year, almost 150,000 of them, with teachers and families, attend productions free or for admissions as low as two or three dollars. There's something for everyone—a play about Winnie-the-Pooh, Native American Indian dances and stories, ballet demonstrations by the Dance Theater of Harlem, "look-ins" on theater performances followed by talks with the actors, designers and sound and light technicians.

Two very special programs for District of Columbia youth are the Arts Enterprise Zone (AEZ) and Cultural Passport Program. The AEZ, in which the Center collaborates with local arts and education organizations, focuses on bringing the arts and artists into schools in neighborhoods where poverty, violence and drug use are commonplace.

With their "Cultural Passports" in hand, District of Columbia youths can take in a wide variety of events all around the city, in theaters, concert halls, museums and even at the zoo. Then, in Culture Clubs back at their schools, they talk over what they've seen and heard, write up their experiences and feelings in special Passport Notebooks and have the satisfaction of knowing that their comments will be considered in future planning of the programs.

One of the Center's biggest, splashiest, most colorful, lively and noisy, community outreach programs is its Open House Arts Festival every fall. It's come one, come all from all over the District, Maryland and Virginia to an afternoon that's part theater, part circus and part county fair complete with story tellers, balloon sculptors, face painters, clowns, magicians, unicyclists, folk dancers and canoe and kayak racers on the Potomac River. The air resounds with music inside and out: classical music, rock, reggae, blues, gospel, opera, classical brass and steel drums, along with swingin' square dancers, dazzling tap dancers and sultry cabaret singers in the Atrium-turned-coffee-house. And there's plenty of traditional festival food—hot 'n spicy barbecue, buttery popcorn, ice cream, giant pretzels, nachos, watermelon and great big sticky clouds of pink cotton candy.

In addition to these local programs, the Center influences national educational programs with a five-day annual Institute called "Performing Art Centers and Schools: Partners in Education," in which educators become enthusiastic students. During the Institute, two-partner teams (one partner representing a community's art center, the other its school system) explore how to create their own arts education programs to help teachers learn more about the arts and acquire skills in teaching them. The program is based on the belief that educating teachers is essential to any effort designed to increase young peoples' knowledge of the arts. The participants come from urban, suburban and rural communities across the country, some from as far away as Kodiak, Alaska.

Through hands-on activities, these teams learn about program models that have been developed and refined by the Kennedy Center over more than 15 years. In one model program teams take part in performance-based events. They have discussions with directors, composers and choreographers, for example, and they attend master classes. In another model program they participate in workshops such as music, dance and storytelling, and they explore how to relate these arts to their schools' curricula. Teams that initiate or expand programs for teachers as a result of what they have learned at the Institute may receive ongoing consultations with the Center's staff.

Other outreach efforts include The Kennedy Center Alliance for Arts Education Network (KCAAEN). This nationwide association of educators, community leaders, concerned citizens and arts organizations works together with the Center to "ensure that the arts are woven into the very fiber of American education." This includes developing and supporting partnerships between schools and cultural institutions, calling public attention to arts programs, sponsoring teacher conferences and offering festivals and performances for young people.

Additionally, the Center offers funding and technical assistance and develops a variety of arts advocacy materials such as position papers, posters and flyers that help promote and publicize the arts. One important aim of the Network is to disseminate information about the educational programs and resources of the Kennedy Center.

Many of the workshops the Center and the National Symphony Orchestra offer to teachers for their professional development are spirited events with an emphasis on "doing." For example, singers and songwriters Kim and Reggie Harris have led hand-clapping, foot-stomping teachers through rousing songs designed to teach youngsters about slaves fleeing to freedom through the underground railroad and of the people of other races who helped them. In another workshop, artist Deanne Collins has had teachers singing, shouting, jumping, spinning and swaying in folk dances from around the world, dances they took back to their students to help them appreciate differences between cultures. In another music-filled session taught by Craig Woodson, designer of musical instruments for young people, teachers made sets of simple instruments such as Arabic drums, Asian reed instruments or Spanish guitars. They then learned to use them to teach music, science and social studies as well as to foster pride in their students' cultural heritage.

In other sessions, teachers have observed first-rate artists such as violinist Pinchas Zukerman or ballet dancer Ross Stretton teaching some of their master classes. By watching and asking questions, teachers learn new approaches to teaching, new ways to make their own classes more innovative and alive. As James Wolfensohn puts it, ". . . watch the creative sparks fly."

The goal of the workshops is admirably summed up in the words of one participant: "As a teacher, the more I know, the more I can give in music, literature and art." Another teacher adds, "And have a good time, too."

For one week every April excitement runs especially high at the Center when the winning productions of the Kennedy Center American College Theater Festival (KC/ACTF) are showcased in the Terrace Theater. The week is the culmination of a year-round program in eight nationwide geographic regions in which the theater departments of colleges and universities compete with productions of their best work. They share experiences and insights with one another and are recognized through awards and scholarships in playwriting, acting, criticism, directing and design. Some 16,000 students in 800 colleges are involved in the program whose goals are to encourage exciting theater work at the college level, to give participants a chance to develop their skills and encourage the production of new plays, experimental works and revitalized classics. The Kennedy Center provides funding and support—and that exciting chance for the regional winners to come to the nation's capital, all expenses paid, and perform in the country's number one performing arts center. For many of these young people the KC/ACTF is their first big step on the way to a professional career in the arts.

"Imagination Celebration" is the colorful name for a network of performing arts festivals offered for young people, free or at low cost, by the Kennedy Center at the Center and at schools and theaters across the nation. Examples of "Imagination Celebration" events are: a musical puppet show for preschoolers called *Dinorock* about the mystery of dinosaur extinction; an adventure story for kindergartners about a magic French horn, told in music and mime by the NSO and Magic Circle Mime Co.; the world premiere of the Kennedy Center's new stage production of *Alice In Wonderland*, directed by Pat Carroll; a musical play called *Beethoven Lives Upstairs*, which introduces grammar school children to classical music performed by the National Symphony Orchestra; and spine-tingling performances of *Tales of Terror from Edgar Allan Poe* for grades seven and above.

Another program, "New Visions/New Voices," works with playwrights and directors encouraging them to create new works especially for young audiences.

Through its educational affiliate, Very Special Arts, founded by Jean Kennedy Smith in 1974, the Center helps make the arts accessible to young people with special needs. One example of this joint effort is Very Special Arts' Young Soloist Program, a yearly competition for musicians under age 25 who have a disability. The winner receives a $5,000 scholarship and an opportunity to play at the Kennedy Center.

Bright, enthusiastic and mostly "twenty-something" is the best description for the every-changing groups of young people who stride around the Center with energy and creativity to burn. They're "The Interns"— no, not characters in a TV soap opera, but on-the-job trainees in the Center's internship program for young people heading for careers in performing arts management and/or arts education. These vital influential future leaders in the arts are the cream of the crop. The Center gives them a good, solid workout during their three- or four-month internship in every office, every program and, seemingly, in every niche and corner of the building.

"Backstage and beyond" describes the Center's educational program aptly titled "Performance Plus." In more than 100 free or low cost popular events audiences meet the actors, dancers, musicians, directors, choreographers, composers and conductors of performances they'll attend. The activities are varied—lectures, discussions, demonstrations, explorations of backstage areas, look-ins at rehearsals and master classes—but all offer important insights into the performing arts.

The National Symphony Orchestra also has many educational activities for both young and old. There are Family Concerts, Young Apprentice Training Programs for students who want to learn about music as a profession, Young Soloists Competitions in which winners perform with the NSO, pre-performance lectures, College Music Fairs at which high school students meet recruiters from conservatories and universities, Career Day panel discussions on careers in music and high-school level orchestral training programs. About 44,000 elementary school children are introduced to symphonic music in the sparkling setting of the Kennedy Center's Concert Hall each year.

To further help youngsters discover the joy of music, the NSO has developed some delightful and imaginative events such as its "Come to the Musical Fair," a time of fun and learning just before a performance. For example, in "Musical Bingo," the recorded sounds of musical instruments take the place of letters and numbers, and children must identify the instruments properly before shouting "bingo!" In a variation of pin-the-tail-on-the-donkey, youngsters pin pictures of musical instruments to their proper positions on an orchestra seating chart.

Kids love to touch things, and kids love zoos. Putting these two loves together the NSO has come up with its wildly popular Instrument Petting Zoo in

At the Instrument Petting Zoo four-year-old Sean adds his vigorous drum beat to the ear-splitting, but joyful din.

which youngsters can "pet" instruments of the orchestra by exploring their nooks, crannies, holes, levers, reeds and strings. They can try to make music of their own by tooting flutes, banging drums, blowing horns, plucking strings, flourishing the bows of violins, cellos and bass viols. The more noise the merrier. The "music" may sound like fog horns or croaky frogs, but there's no telling how many hidden musical talents are awakened at this "zoo."

Adults are not forgotten in this educational potpourri. The NSO invites senior citizens to special open rehearsals. It also sponsors a series of free lectures at libraries, provides recorded program notes for concert goers with impaired vision and offers NSO subscribers free audio cassettes of pre-performance commentary to enhance their enjoyment of the evening's music.

For information about any of the Center's and NSO's education programs, write to the Education Department, The Kennedy Center, Washington, D.C., 20566 and mark the envelope to the attention of the program in which you're interested. To speak with the manager of any one of the programs dial (202)416-8800.

As the resident opera company of the Kennedy Center (an honorary position which brings a certain cachet but no financial support), the Washington Opera shares the Center's aims of producing the highest quality work, encouraging new talent and developing innovative educational programs, many of which are co-sponsored by the Kennedy Center Education Department.

The most ambitious of these ventures to make opera user-friendly is a four-part program that involves volunteers and singers. In part one, volunteer docents visit schools to talk about an opera that will be produced that season. Children get a chance to hold a conductor's baton, try on costumes and listen to a little of the music. Part two takes some of the singers to the classrooms for free-wheeling talks with the youngsters about their roles and their lives as opera singers. Also, they act and sing an excerpt or two from the opera and answer a barrage of questions. In part three, the children troop down to the Center for a fascinating behind-the-scenes "Look-In." They learn how special effects are created, what stagehands do and how the orchestra and singers work together. The finale of the "Look-In" is a scene from the opera complete with music, costumes and full make-up. Approximately 6,000 students, from fourth grade through high school, attend these "Look-Ins" every year.

Part four of the program, called Family Night at the Opera, is for a few representative children and their families. These lucky ones are invited to a full performance at the Kennedy Center. The youngsters not only glimpse the magic of the theater, but they enhance their self-esteem by sharing their new opera knowledge with their families.

Additionally, the opera offers educational materials for classroom use and sponsors the exciting Student Dress Rehearsal Program in which more than 1,500 high school and university students are invited to the Center annually to see opera at its grandest.

For youngsters who are disabled the "Look-In" program provides audio-describers, sign language interpreters, study guides in braille and large print and "hands on" sessions in which children "see" props and costumes through their sense of touch.

Adult education is equally active and imaginative and designed to meet the needs of both novices and experienced opera lovers with a variety of symposia, backstage tours, technical demonstrations, pre-performance lectures, "Meet the Performers" sessions and round-table discussions. In addition, a handsome, award-winning Washington Opera magazine highlights the current productions with summaries of the opera plots and profiles of the singers. With all this to stimulate and educate them, Washington audiences have become highly "opera-knowledgeable" and ardent boosters of their opera "home team."

In a January 1992, editorial titled "Kennedy Center Kids," *The Washington Post* noted the changes set in motion by Chairman Wolfensohn—the new aggressiveness in commissioning new works, the "flooding" of the Center with youngsters on arts education field trips and providing follow-up classroom materials.

"If school arts budgets continue to be cut as they have been," the editorial stated, "the task falls to places like the Kennedy Center for creating their own future audience. In the search for roles for a national arts center to fulfill, Mr. Wolfensohn could hardly have hit on a better one."

11 *What They Do for Love*

They come for love, certainly not for fame or money. Kennedy Center volunteers come through rain and snow, through Washington's infamous heat and humidity, through snarled traffic and circuitous routes around the presidential cavalcades, marches, demonstrations and other gatherings-of-the-thousands that are part of life in the nation's capital. They are over 1,800 strong and they'll tackle just about anything that needs to be done. The volunteer men and women who support the Kennedy Center, the NSO and Washington Opera bring their time and talent, their incredible energy and resourcefulness.

Among these volunteers are the Friends of the Kennedy Center, approximately 650 arts-loving people who not only make annual monetary gifts, but give of their time, too—about 76,000 hours a year, valued at well over a million dollars. The Friends trace their roots back to 1965 when they were founded by ardent performing arts supporter Lily Polk Guest, who is honored with a bronze plaque at the tour desk.

The Friends' first major volunteer effort was to raise matching funds for the Center's construction. When the building was completed, they moved in to help in other practical ways—with continuing financial support, but also with time and talent in helping to administer programs and to provide services for the visitors who came by the tens of thousands to see this grand, new memorial.

The first person that most tourists meet at the Center is a Friend. He or she may be a volunteer at the public information center and his/her pleasure will be to answer such questions as What's playing on stage? How high are these ceilings? Is there a restaurant? Where are the restrooms? Friends who serve as volunteer tour guides field the same questions and often more: How do they clean the chandeliers? How much did all this cost? Still other Friends can be seen clerking in either of two inviting shops selling gifts that range from 25¢ novelty pencils to $700 sculptures.

These are the most visible positions, but behind the scenes scores more volunteers work in the Performing Arts Library and the Administrative Offices doing yeoman duty typing, answering phones, filing, stuffing envelopes, clipping and routing arts-oriented newspaper stories, working on fund-raising and membership drives, assisting people with disabilities and administering the program that the Center is particularly proud of—the Specially Priced Ticket (SPT) program. Since its opening in 1971, the Center has made half-price tickets available to some 100,000 senior citizens, students, persons with permanent disabilities, enlisted military personnel (E-1 to E-4) and persons with fixed incomes.

In specialized areas the Center makes good use of the volunteers' professional talents. They work as research and public relations assistants, project organizers and training program developers. Once a year, many of these behind-the-scene workers come out into the sunshine, literally, to welcome more than 25,000 visitors, most of them children, to the Center's Open House Arts Festival. New talents among the volunteers are discovered and new jobs are learned: operating elevators; directing foot traffic; reuniting "lost and found" children and parents; showing youngsters how to blow into a sax, rat-a-tat a drum or slide a trombone; painting colorful flowers and stars on toddlers' cheeks; selling fund-raiser T-shirts; setting up equipment at dawn's early light and taking it down at dusk; hauling trash bags and even prancing through the halls in sweltering hot clown and bunny rabbit costumes. It's all in a volunteer's job description.

Besides the 25,000 people who swarm through the Center during Open House, every year more than 100,000 visitors take hour-long guided tours that are offered free every day of the week. The tours start in the Level A Tour Lobby. Before heading out through the Center with a tour guide, visitors can watch a short introductory film, *A Place For The Spirit*, narrated by

Jean Stapleton and captioned for people with impaired hearing. (Other considerations for people with disabilities include "listening enhancement systems" in the theaters, sign-language interpreted and audio-described performances and tours designed especially to introduce people with disabilities to the Center and its artwork.)

In April 1991 the work of the volunteers was officially recognized in a White House ceremony when the Friends were one of only 19 volunteer organizations in the country to receive the President's Volunteer Action Award for exemplary voluntary achievements in their communities. In the Hall of States, etched large in the marble, is an acknowledgment of the Friends' years of "dedicated service since 1965."

Up at the "Wash Op," the volunteers' fond nickname for the Washington Opera, some 140 men and women—and a teen-ager or two—put in 12,000 hours of work every year stuffing envelopes, clipping and routing opera-related newspaper stories, updating mailing lists and making computer entries. They're known affectionately by the opera staff as the "office rescue team," and their work represents a gift equivalent to $200,000.

Over in Alexandria, Virginia, in the Opera's wardrobe and "props" warehouse, volunteers skilled with needle and thread patiently stitch miles of ruffles and hems on elaborate costumes. Other "outside jobs" by volunteers include transporting visiting singers to and from airports and to schools for their talks with young people. Many volunteers also visit classrooms to prepare students for youth performances at the Center.

If the largess of "snacks" that they tote in for everyone to nibble on is any criterion, volunteers must inherently be sharers. Up at the Wash Op they feast on chocolate cake, pumpkin bread, even hot pots of chili and peanut soup. And down in their snug little coffee lounge, the Friends' tour guides and gift shop clerks ply one another with homemade cakes, cookies and mini-sandwiches.

The NSO has its own cadre of dedicated volunteers known as the Women's Committee for the National Symphony Orchestra. In June 1941, a newspaper photo of the Committee's luncheon meeting to adopt articles of organization was captioned, "Women Meet To Aid Music." At that time, 19 women were on the committee. Today, 1,050 women continue to promote the NSO by holding receptions for guest artists, assisting in ticket sales, doing clerical tasks, soliciting donations and holding special fund-raising projects. They have raised $4 million in 20 years through the Decorator's Show House, held each October.

The Women's Committee also operates the Welcome Center in the Concert Hall foyer before concerts and at intermissions. They answer questions about the concert season, special events and activities to support the orchestra. In fact, the Women's Committee does everything involved with symphonic music except actually plucking strings and blowing into mouthpieces (though many of the volunteers are musicians who show youngsters how to play at the popular Instrument Petting Zoo).

Besides the Petting Zoo, other educational projects of the Committee include the annual Young People's Concerts for grades three through six. Committee members handle reservations and monitor the youngsters (about 40,000 every year) during the concerts. Working as docents in the weeks before the concert, they fan out into the schools to prepare the children for what they'll hear. Telling stories about the music and playing sample tunes, they spark the youngsters' interest. It's all part of the goal of building audiences for the future.

By contributing an average of over $200,000 to the orchestra every year, the Women's Committee has been able to endow the Principal Oboe Chair, sponsor the sixth week of the orchestra's concert season, sponsor a guest conductor and contribute to several of the orchestra's educational programs.

Another group, of both men and women, called FANS (Friends Assisting the National Symphony), also promotes the National Symphony and raises funds by sponsoring events that feature orchestra members. For example, under a program entitled "NSO At Home", musicians contribute their time and talents to an evening of chamber music in private residences. A caterer may donate dinner for the occasion. Those who attend pay an average of $50 for the evening. Other events may be designed around concerts, such as a picnic before a performance at Wolf Trap Farm Park, located in the nearby Virginia countryside.

Once a year the FANS hold a larger, more formal fund-raising event that focuses on a concert at the Center. One example is an evening called "In Celebration" for which people donate dinner parties in their homes for about 20 guests including a celebrity who may be from any field including music, politics and the press. As many as 12 dinner parties may be held on one evening. After cocktails and dinner in the donors' homes, the guests, who pay for the evening, attend a concert at the Kennedy Center followed by dessert and champagne in the Atrium.

FANS also help staff the Welcome Center in the Concert Hall foyer.

Setting the pace for volunteerism at the Center is its chairman, James Wolfensohn, who has voluntarily contributed his talent and leadership since his election to the post in March 1990. An investment banker, Mr. Wolfensohn also knows and loves the arts. He is a skilled cellist and has a daughter who is a professional pianist. He adamantly believes, constantly reiterates, and has fixed as the Center's goal the belief that the performing arts are not optional extras in our lives. They must be an integral part of every child's education, he feels, to free the child's creative spirit.

Mr. Wolfensohn's dream and goal for the Center—and for the arts-enriched lives of all Americans—is at the heart of a quote by President Kennedy that is etched into the marble on the River Terrace side of the building:

"I am certain that after the dust of centuries has passed over our cities, we, too, will be remembered not for our victories or defeats in battle or in politics, but for our contribution to the human spirit."

Practical Facts About
The Kennedy Center

How To Get There

By public transportation: If using the *Metrorail*, get off at the Foggy Bottom-George Washington University station at 23rd and I Streets. From there it is a 7- to 10-minute walk to the Center via New Hampshire Avenue. *Metrobusses* also serve the Center. Use routes 46, 80, L-4, M-5 or M-12. For more detailed information and specific time tables call Metro Information at (202) 637-7000 (TT 638-3780).

By car: There is parking in the Center's underground garage. Its entrance is on the south side of the building. If you are approaching from the south on Rock Creek Parkway, take the Kennedy Center exit. It leads directly into the garage. If you are approaching from the Foggy Bottom area, take New Hampshire Avenue toward the Watergate. Stay on New Hampshire, past the Watergate complex, and up the hill in front of the Center. Continue past the entrances to the Halls of States and Nations. The road goes to the end of the building and makes a righthand U-turn into the garage. There is additional parking at two nearby buildings, the Watergate at 600 New Hampshire Avenue and Columbia Plaza at 2300 Virginia Avenue. There is free shuttle service to and from the Columbia Plaza for evening and week-end performances. Persons who come to the Center to buy tickets at the box office between 10:00 A.M. and 6:00 P.M. Monday through Saturday and NOON–6:00 P.M. Sundays and holidays may have their parking tickets validated at the box office for 60 minutes of free parking in the Center's garage.

Specially Priced Tickets (SPT)

The Kennedy Center has the nation's largest half-price ticket program which is made possible by private donations and the voluntary participation of the organizations which present the shows. The half-price tickets are available for most performances to people over age 65, people with permanent disabilities, enlisted military personnel in grades El-E4, full-time students from kindergarten through graduate school and people on fixed, low incomes. Proof of eligibility must be shown in the form of school, military or permanent disability ID cards, driver's licenses or human resources cards.

A limited number of SPTs may be bought in advance at the box office or by mail. Depending on availability, SPTs may also be bought on the day of the performance beginning at NOON for matinees and at 6:00 P.M. for evening performances from the box office in the Hall of Nations. For more information and to find out if tickets to specific performances are available, call (202)467-4600 or 1(800)444-1324, TT (202)416-8524.

Restaurants

1. The formal Roof Terrace Restaurant serves lunch on matinee days from 11:30 A.M. to 3:00 P.M. and dinner on performance evenings from 5:50 P.M. to 9:00 P.M. Monday through Saturday. On Sundays, it serves a popular brunch buffet from 11:30 A.M. to 3:00 P.M. For reservations call (202)416-8555.
2. The Hors D'Oeuvrerie, adjacent to the Roof Terrace Restaurant, serves cocktails and light food from 5:00 P.M. until a half hour after the curtain comes down on the last performance.
3. The Encore Cafe (self-service), open from 11:00 A.M. to 8:00 P.M. daily, offers informal food such as pizza, chili, salads and sandwiches. All three restaurants are on the Roof Terrace level on the south (Hall of Nations) side of the building.
4. Food carts in the Grand Foyer offer sandwiches, espresso, cappuchino and sweets before performances and during intermission.

Kennedy Center Memberships

Donors of $50 or more become "Stars" of the Kennedy Center while donors of $1,000 and higher become members of "The Circles." The contributions, which are tax-deductible, support the Special Price Ticket program and the myriad performances for young people that have been described earlier. All members receive special benefits such as advance ticket purchasing priority, advance editions of *The Kennedy Center News Magazine* and discounts in the Gift Shops. There are many other benefits depending on the level of contribution. You may join at any time, or receive membership information, by writing to The Development Office, The Kennedy Center, Washington, D.C. 20566-0003.

Tours

Free, hour-long tours are given from 10:00 A.M. to 1:00 P.M. daily except Christmas Day and New Year's Day. The guides are volunteers who are Friends of the Kennedy Center.

Daily "Congressional Tours" are also available. They cover the same territory as the regular tours. The difference is that they require a pass from your congressman's office, and they start at 9:30 A.M., a half hour before the Center officially opens. They're handy for tourists who want to get an early start on sightseeing. Bring your pass to the entrance of the Hall of States for a 9:30 A.M. admittance.

Large groups wanting to take a tour at a specific time between 10:00 A.M. and 1:00 P.M. may make advance reservations by calling (202)416-8340.

Pamphlets for a Self-Guided Tour are available at the Public Information Center in the Hall of States. The self-guided tour covers the main hallways and Grand Foyer, but theaters and lounges may be seen only on an "official" guided tour.

Public Information Center

The volunteers at this desk in the Hall of States are equipped to answer virtually all questions about the Center, performance schedules, tour bus routes and the location of sightseeing areas around town. The PIC is open from 10:00 A.M. to 9:00 P.M. daily. Tel. (202)416-8340. For information on becoming a volunteer call the Coordinator of Volunteers, at (202)416-8304.

Educational Programs

For information on professional development opportunities for teachers and performances for school groups, call or write The Education Department, The Kennedy Center, Washington, D.C. 20566-0004. Tel. (202)416-8800 (TT 416-8822).

Performing Arts Library

On the Roof Terrace level, the library is open to the public from NOON to 5:00 P.M. Monday through Friday. See Chapter 6 for description of library facilities.

Facilities for People with Disabilities

1. There are parking spaces for cars with handicapped stickers in the Center's garage.
2. Wheelchairs are available and should be reserved in advance by calling (202)416-8340/5340 (TT 416-8524).
3. There is an excellent wireless, infrared listening enhancement system for performances in all the theaters. It is free of charge. Simply leave an ID with the usher when you pick up the headphone at the special desk in the Hall of States.
4. Many performances are sign-language interpreted or audio-described. The times and dates of these performances are listed in the monthly *Kennedy Center News Magazine* which is mailed to members of the Center's "Stars" program. Copies are also available on the counter at the Main Box Office in the Hall of States.
5. A public TT is located at the Public Information Center in the Hall of States.
6. If you have questions about facilities for people with disabilities, please call (202)416-8340 or (202)416-8727 (TT 416-8728).

Gifts From Other Countries

Africa: *African Lounge, the donation of many African nations.*

Argentina: *Oil paintings by Raquel Forner in box tier of Opera House; bronze sculpture by Libero Badii on first tier of Concert Hall.*

Australia: *Seven tapestries by John Coburn in South Gallery on Roof Terrace level.*

Austria: *Lobmeyr crystal chandelier and light fixtures for Opera House.*

Belgium: *Mirrors for Grand Foyer and Opera House.*

Brazil: *Fiberwork sculpture by Jacques Douchez in stairwell of Hall of States.*

Bulgaria: *Sculpture by Professor V. Minekov.*

Canada: *Stage curtain for Eisenhower Theater.*

Colombia: *Metal sculpture by Eduardo Ramirez on lawn of south circular drive.*

Cyprus: *Ancient amphora for box tier of Eisenhower Theater.*

Czechoslovakia: *Two tapestries by Alfons Mucha.*

Denmark: *Porcelain wall relief by Inge-Lise Koefoed for Concert Hall lobby.*

Egypt: *Alabaster vase, circa 2600 B.C. for box tier of Eisenhower Theater.*

Finland: *Chinaware for the Roof Terrace restaurants.*

France: *Two tapestries by Henri Matisse and two bronze sculptures by Henri Laurens for box tier of Opera House.*

Germany: *Sculpted bronze panels by Jurgen Weber on front plaza opposite entrances.*

Great Britain: *Bronze sculpture by Dame Barbara Hepworth for box tier of Concert Hall.*

Greece: *Bronze cast of ancient statue of Poseidon for box tier of Opera House.*

India: *Twenty brass planters for indoor greenery.*

Iran: *Two silk and wool rugs for anteroom of South Opera Lounge.*

Ireland: *Waterford crystal chandelier and four sconces for South Opera Lounge.*

Israel: *Artwork and furnishings for Concert Hall Lounge on box tier.*

Italy: *Cararra marble, cut to specifications, for exterior and interior of building.*

Japan: *Opera House stage curtain; Terrace Theater, as Bicentennial gift to America.*

Luxembourg: *Marble sculpture by Lucien Wercollier for box tier of Concert Hall.*

Malaysia: *Shadow puppets from Ramayana epics.*

Mexico: *Two tapestries by Leonardo Nierman.*

Morocco: *Black and white wool carpets for North and South Galleries.*

Netherlands: *17th-century oil painting by P.G. van Roestraeten for anteroom of South Opera Lounge.*

Norway: *Eleven Hadelands crystal chandeliers for Concert Hall.*

Pakistan: *Two Bokhara rugs for South Opera Lounge.*

Peru: *Painting by Antonio Maro in stairwell of Hall of Nations.*

Portugal: *Planters made of ceramic tiles by Mario de Silva in North and South Galleries.*

Spain: *Two tapestries reproduced from paintings by Goya in South Opera Lounge; bronze and marble statue of Don Quixote by Aurelio Teno for east lawn.*

Sri Lanka: *Two handcrafted standing brass oil lamps for anteroom of South Opera Lounge.*

Sweden: *Eighteen Orrefors crystal chandeliers for Grand Foyer.*

Switzerland: *Metal wall sculpture for lobby of Concert Hall.*

Thailand: *Thai silk for furnishings.*

Tunisia: *Reproduction of 3rd century mosaic for Roof Terrace.*

Turkey: *Porcelain vases designed by Muhsin Demironat.*

Uruguay: *Metal sculpture by Alfredo Halegua for north lawn.*

Yugoslavia: *Tapestries by Jagoda Buic and Matega Rocci.*

(For several reasons, including preservation, restoration and renovation, not all gifts are displayed at all times.)

Hall of States

Flags of the 50 states are hung in the order in which they entered the nation. Flags of the District of Columbia and five Territories are also in historical order.

Grand Foyer

28 Texas, December 28, 1845
27 Florida, March 3, 1845
26 Michigan, January 26, 1837
25 Arkansas, June 15, 1836
24 Missouri, August 10, 1821
23 Maine, March 15, 1820
22 Alabama, December 14, 1819
21 Illinois, December 3, 1818
20 Mississippi, December 10, 1817
19 Indiana, December 11, 1816
18 Louisiana, April 30, 1812
17 Ohio, March 1, 1803
16 Tennessee, June 1, 1796
15 Kentucky, June 1, 1792
14 Vermont, March 4, 1791
13 Rhode Island, May 29, 1790
12 North Carolina, November 21, 1789
11 New York, July 26, 1788
10 Virginia, June 25, 1788
9 New Hampshire, June 21, 1788
8 South Carolina, May 23, 1788
7 Maryland, April 28, 1788
6 Massachusetts, February 6, 1788
5 Connecticut, January 9, 1788
4 Georgia, January 2, 1788
3 New Jersey, December 18, 1787
2 Pennsylvania, December 12, 1787
1 Delaware, December 7, 1787

29 Iowa, December 28, 1846
30 Wisconsin, May 29, 1848
31 California, September 9, 1850
32 Minnesota, May 11, 1858
33 Oregon, February 14, 1859
34 Kansas, January 29, 1861
35 West Virginia, June 20, 1863
36 Nevada, October 31, 1864
37 Nebraska, March 1, 1867
38 Colorado, August 1, 1876
39 North Dakota, November 2, 1889
40 South Dakota, November 2, 1889
41 Montana, November 8, 1889
42 Washington, November 11, 1889
43 Idaho, July 3, 1890
44 Wyoming, July 10, 1890
45 Utah, January 5, 1896
46 Oklahoma, November 16, 1907
47 New Mexico, January 6, 1912
48 Arizona, February 14, 1912
49 Alaska, January 3, 1959
50 Hawaii, August 21, 1959
District of Columbia, December 1, 1800
Puerto Rico, December 10, 1898
Guam, December 10, 1898
American Samoa, July 14, 1904
Virgin Islands, March 31, 1917
Northern Marianas, November 3, 1986

Front Plaza Entrance to Hall of States

Hall of Nations

Flags of nations where the U.S. has diplomatic missions (as of 1994). Hung in alpbabetical order beginning on right as you face the plaza entrance.

United States	Congo	Hungary	Nauru
Albania	Costa Rica	Iceland	Nepal
Algeria	Cote D'Ivoire	India	Netherlands
Argentina	Cyprus	Indonesia	New Zealand
Armenia	Czechoslovakia	Ireland	Nicaragua
Australia	Denmark	Italy	Niger
Austria	Djibouti	Jamaica	Nigeria
Bahamas	Dominica	Japan	Norway
Bahrain	Dominican	Jordan	Oman
Bangladesh	Republic	Kenya	Pakistan
Barbados	Ecuador	Kiribati	Panama
Belgium	Egypt	Korea	Papua New
Belize	El Salvador	Kuwait	Guinea
Benin	Equatorial	Laos	Paraguay
Bolivia	Guinea	Latvia	Peru
Botswana	Estonia	Lebanon	Philippines
Brazil	Ethiopia	Lesotho	Poland
Brunei	Fiji	Liberia	Portugal
Bulgaria	Finland	Lithuania	Qatar
Burkina Faso	France	Luxembourg	Romania
Burma	Gabon	Madagascar	Russia
(Myanman)	Gambia	Malawi	Rwanda
Burundi	Germany	Malaysia	Saint Lucia
Byelarus	Ghana	Maldives	St. Vincent
Cambodia	Greece	Mali	& the
Cameroon	Grenada	Malta	Grenadines
Canada	Guatemala	Marshall Islands	Sao Tome and
Cape Verde	Guinea	Mauritania	Principe
Central African	Guinea-Bissau	Mauritius	Saudia Arabia
Republic	Guyana	Mexico	Senegal
Chad	Haiti	Micronesia	Seychelles
Chile	Holy See	Mongolia	Sierra Leone
China	(Vatican)	Morocco	Singapore
Colombia	Honduras	Mozambique	Solomon Islands
Comoros	Hong Kong	Namibia	Somalia

Hall of Nations (cont.)

South Africa
Spain
Sri Lanka
Sudan
Suriname
Swaziland
Sweden
Switzerland
Syria

Tanzania
Thailand
Togo
Tonga
Trinidad and
Tobago
Tunisia
Turkey
Tuvalu

Uganda
Ukraine
United Arab
Emirates
United
Kingdom
Uruguay
Vanuatu

Venezuela
Western Samoa
Yemen
Yugoslavia
Zaire
Zambia
Zimbabawe
United Nations

Acknowledgments

When I began work on this book, I didn't realize how many people I'd need to call on for assistance. I found out quickly. There were dozens—dozens of helpful people whom I am very pleased to acknowledge here. I only regret the lack of space to list them individually. Everyone I talked to, for a few minutes or a few hours, was willing to share whatever he or she knew about the Kennedy Center. Each one confirmed what I already suspected—that "theater people" are exceptionally nice.

Naturally, there are a few individuals and several office staffs to whom I want to give an extra word of thanks, beginning with Larry Wilker, President of the Kennedy Center. His immediate response of interest and support re-ignited my zest for the project at a time when my enthusiasm was running low. I was also greatly helped by the Center's Media Relations Department headed by Tiki Davies; by Geraldine Otremba, Director, Government Liaison; by the staff of the Performing Arts Library, especially Vicky Wulff; the Center's Education Office; the staff of the Friends of the Kennedy Center; the personnel of the National Park Service and the U.S. Park Police; Leo Gallenstein, Supervisor of Theater Operations, Maintenance Department; the Public Relations Departments of the National Symphony, Washington Opera and The American Film Institute as well as the theater managers who enthusiastically escorted me through their theaters and the backstage nooks and crannies.

Despite incredibly busy schedules, both Robert Berks who sculpted the Center's bust of President Kennedy, and Dr. Cyril Harris who designed the Center's acoustics, gave generously of their time and provided photos and written materials. I thank them sincerely.

And I surely can't forget the unflagging enthusiasm and help of my cohorts, the dedicated crew of Wednesday tour guides and Public Information Center volunteers.

Thanks also to my two main photographers, Carol Pratt and Lise Metzger, talented women, whose striking images—and occasional humorous ones—offer fresh and imaginative perspectives of the Center and its art works.

An especially big "thank you" to my friend Julie Glass whose professional opinion gave me the impetus to follow through on my idea for this book and whose advice led me to just the right person for the subject— Evelyn Metzger who has become a friend as well as my understanding, enthusiastic publisher. I am most grateful to Kathi Shull for her excellent, sensitive editing of my manuscript, and also to the other staff members of EPM Publications, Inc.

Lastly, but with great feeling, I thank my cheerleaders, Conny and El, and my husband who was my greatest moral support and my first proofreader and editor. I thank him also for scrupulously (well, almost) obeying the "Do Not Disturb" sign on my office door.

Sources

The Washington Post, September 5–10, 1971; October 29, 1975; January 29, 1979; September 26 and 29, 1979.

The Washington Evening Star, September 5–10, 1971; April 24, 1972.

John F. Kennedy Center For Performing Arts by Brendan Gill, Harry N. Abrams, Inc. publisher, 1981.

Life Magazine, June 11, 1971.

Miracle On The Potomac by Ralph E. Becker, Bartleby Press, 1990.

The Great Kennedy Center Rip-off by Fred Blumenthal, *Parade Magazine,* March 12, 1972.

A Dream Realized by Jacqueline Kennedy Onassis, *Ladies' Home Journal,* September 1971.

Edward Marshall Boehm, advertisement for Boehm of Malvern England Ltd., *Country Life,* July 7, 1972.

My Recollections of the "Picasso of Porcelains", Edward Boehm by Meredith Havens, *The Antique Trader Dubuque, December 1972.*

Mosby, The Kennedy Center Cat by Beppie Noyes, Acropolis Books, LTD, 1978.

Records of Columbia Historical Society of Washington, D.C., 50th volume:

The JFK Center: From Dream to Reality by Roger Meersman, p. 525.

The Kennedy Center: Early Years of Operation by Roger Meersman, p. 589.

The New Yorker: A Quiet Man by Bruce Bliven, Jr., June 17, 1972; *Annals of Architecture—A Better Sound* by Bruce Bliven, Jr., November 8, 1976.

Acoustical Design of the John F. Kennedy Center for the Performing Arts by Cyril M. Harris, *The Journal of The Acoustical Society of America*, January 1972.

The Nation's Stage, ad supplement of Kennedy Center in *The Business Week 1000 Issue*, April 1992, text by Thor Eckert, Jr.

The Kennedy Center News Magazine, issue of December 1993–January 1994.

Index

About the Author

Barbara Bradlyn Morris of Alexandria, VA, has free-lanced articles, primarily on travel and food, for 20 years for such publications as *The Washington Post, Los Angeles Times, New York Newsday, House Beautiful, Bon Appetit, Army/Navy/Air Force Times, Pacific Stars and Stripes* and *Far East Traveler.* Earlier, she worked in public relations in New York City and during her tours of duty as a naval officer in Florida, Hawaii and Washington, D.C.

She and her husband Ward, a retired Navy Captain, are ardent theater and music lovers, and long-time Friends of the Kennedy Center. Having served as a volunteer tour guide since 1991, Mrs. Morris knows the Kennedy Center from its orchestra pits to its terrace top and shares her knowledge with infectious joy.

Photographers

Carol Pratt specializes in portraiture and performance photography. Her clients include The John F. Kennedy Center for the Performing Arts, the Washington Opera, The Wolf Trap Foundation, Arena Stage, Time-Warner and the Oratorio Society of Washington. She received a degree in business management at James Madison University and studied photography at the Northern Virginia Community College. Her work has appeared in *The Washington Post* and *Washington Times, New York Times, Washington Opera Magazine* and *Time Magazine.*

Her photographs appear on the Cover and pages 2, 30, 32, 34, 42, 49, 50, 51, 52, 54, 60, 70, 78 and 90.

Lise Metzger, a fine art and commercial photographer, has won recognition for her portraiture in *Communication Arts* and *Graphis* magazines, among others. In 1993 she won awards from the *Photo District News*/Nikon Self-Promotion Awards Competition and from the Washington Arts Directors Club. She received her B.A. from Johns Hopkins University and her M.F.A. from the University of Delaware, and has taught photography at Lorton Reformatory and Gallaudet University.

Her photographs appear on pages 8, 22, 28, 36, 38, 40, 46, 48, 73, 107 and 118.

Photographs on pages 10 and 24 are through the courtesy of Robert Berks.

The photograph on page 84 is by Joan Marcus.

Floor Plan of The John F. Kennedy Center

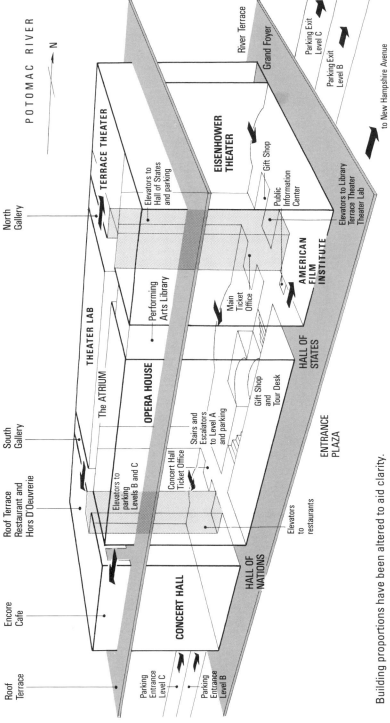

Building proportions have been altered to aid clarity.